MW01628087

Sam,

Best wishes for your success and abundance.

Ron

Other books by Ron Willingham

How to Speak So People Will Listen

Life Is What You Make It

The Best Seller

Integrity Selling

When Good Isn't Good Enough

Hey, I'm The Customer

The People Principle

Integrity Selling For The 21st Century

Integrity Service

The Inner Game of Selling

The You, You Never Knew

The Ten Laws of Wealth & Abundance

Wherein are Reveal'd the Secrets of Enjoying a Plentiful Supply of Money

RON WILLINGHAM

WWW.THETENLAWSOFWEALTH.COM
IS A DIVISION OF
LIFESCRIPT LEARNING, LLC

The Ten Laws of Wealth & Abundance

Andrew Baldwin, the main character of this book is fictional, and any resemblance to actual persons is coincidental. Many of the sayings and examples of Benjamin Franklin are based upon historical facts.

First printing, 2007
Printed in the United States of America
Book and cover design by Gladys Pinkerton

ISBN 13 978-0-9797061-0-3
ISBN 10 0-9797061-0-6

Dedication

TO THE MEMORY OF
W. CLEMENT STONE.

He was my Benjamin Franklin.
His consuming passion was to make
the world a better place in which to live.
This little book is my way of
keeping his dream alive.

If you would not be forgotten
As soon as you are dead and rotten,
Either write things worth the reading,
Or do things worth the writing.

— *Poor Richard's Almanack*

PROLOGUE

The Ten Laws of Wealth & Abundance

Andrew Baldwin
Philadelphia
August, 1820

As I stand looking out the front window of my spacious library, I have an unfettered view of my sprawling estate as it rolls down to the freshwater Schuylkill River. I see before me dozens of field hands working my orchards and fields. I admire the beautiful roses and hyacinths carefully laid in rows surrounding the grand entry. Giant black oaks, maples, and sycamores flank the curving road as it winds from the river to the house. What a beautiful sight!

I turn and survey the treasures of art and literacy that adorn my library walls and bookshelves. On my desk is one of my most prized possessions, the original manuscript of Samuel Richardson's *Pamela*, the first novel ever published in Colonial America.

On a nearby console are twenty-five leather-bound volumes of *Poor Richard's Almanacks*, each signed and presented to me by my mentor, teacher, and friend, Benjamin Franklin. Oh, what wonderful memories I have of him, his genius, his wisdom, his wit and his willingness to spend time with me and assist me in learning the way to wealth.

I never tire of looking at the beautiful Thomas Gainesborough painting that hangs over the mantel in this room. I purchased it in London in 1795, just seven years after the death of the great painter. Already the value of his work has increased many times over.

On another wall is a framed original ticket to the coronation celebration of George II of England, another gift from Dr. Franklin. It reads: Coronation Ticket, Westminster Abbey, September 27, 1761. This ticket was given to Dr. Franklin when he attended the coronation in person.

All these things keep me ever mindful of and grateful for my good fortune and wealth that extended into many areas. I owned stores and buildings and property. My ships brought back fine English linens and china, along with Scottish woolens and beautiful crystal from Sweden. They carried exquisite silks from the Orient, gleaming gemstones from Brazil, tea and spices from Ceylon and India. We traded for these with tobacco, cotton, gold, silver, indigo, and fine furs. My vast warehouses were filled with merchandise for the townspeople who frequented my stores and shops.

Now in my waning years, I am able to spend much of my time with various charities—hospitals, libraries, and universities. Remembering my past years of poverty, I neglect not the poor.

Yes, I do not want for material comforts but have them in abundance. However, I constantly remind myself that it was not always this way. Indeed, in my youth I knew extreme poverty, hardly ever knowing what it felt like to have a full stomach or to be warm at night. And I was surrounded by people who carried no hope of ever rising above the low state they were in, until I, too, felt hopeless.

I wallowed in that hopelessness through my youth, until the fateful day when I met a very famous man who helped me discover the way to wealth, the laws that govern the accumulation of money. What he helped me learn changed my life forever, as it can the life of anyone who makes practical application of these few basic prosperity principles.

These are the laws and lessons that I now share with you, dear reader, in the pages which follow. These are the foundational principles which will guide you down the path to abundance, that is, if you choose to embrace them and apply them to your own life.

I have learned many lessons in my long, good life. I have learned that knowledge can be taught, but not wisdom. Wisdom, or the sensible application of knowledge, must be acquired. It is not knowledge that brings prosperity and fulfillment, but the judicial use of wisdom. Wealth without wisdom corrupts and destroys; wealth with wisdom ennobles and beautifies.

In my quest for wealth and abundance I have known many seasons—good times, bad times, much happiness and love, deep sadness and emptiness. There were times when unbelievable fortunes were showered upon me. There were other occasions when deep emotional hurts ravaged me to the extent I thought that any hope of a happy life had indeed ended. One of these was the loss of two unborn children. Then there was the blackest day of my life when a drunken carriage driver crushed the body of the most beautiful gift that God had bestowed upon me. The pain, the agony, the anger that then filled my soul left it irreparably scarred forever, leaving me to painfully search for deeper meaning and purpose.

In time I learned that wealth and abundance are not measured in possessions and money but in relationships, values and principles; in what we give, not what we get.

But I am getting ahead of myself, as you will surely discover as you read all the pages of this little book.

Before you begin I must warn you. Simply reading this book, even learning the principles contained herein, will do you little good without action and application.

It is through recognizing successful principles in my writings, relating them to your own life, and then developing habits of action that you will begin to discover your own way to wealth. Permit me to emphasize that it's not the knowing of the prosperity principles of which I write, success is enjoyed only in the practice!

Most importantly, I must emphasize that I am still challenged by the concepts that I will share with you. Through the years I have discovered that they can be understood and practiced on many levels. The more I have learned about them, the more I have learned there is to be learned.

So, I challenge you not to quickly read The Ten Laws and say to yourself, "I already know these to be valuable." Thinking this, you then put the book down. You then fail to discover the deeper principles that cause true prosperity and abundance to flow fully through your life.

What a tragedy this would be, for with diligence and sincere searching you will unearth the awareness of what causes genuine success. You will find that these simple principles are well hidden from most people who tragically look in the wrong places.

You will delight in the knowledge that wealth and abundance are enjoyed in many dimensions. They appear because those simple laws have been practiced. But, it's the formation of deeper values, self-beliefs, and character that give them foundation, without which enduring success is not possible.

Yes, I have observed that what appears to be good fortune or luck is but the result of strong habits that are well formed into a person's values, self-beliefs, and character.

I have witnessed, over and over, how true abundance is elusive, and escapes those who do not give sincere attention to these foundational personal qualities.

So, I encourage you, dear reader, to read this little book through, then come back and spend a week in each chapter. Reread the chapter several times during the week. Identify ideas of action and practice them. Then go to the next chapter the following week, and continue through the whole of the book.

Continue to follow these suggestions and you will forge, in the crucible of your life experiences, strengths, knowledge and wisdom which will surely plant the seeds of prosperity and abundance in your life.

You will indeed discover your own way to wealth.

THE TEN LAWS OF WEALTH AND ABUNDANCE

1.

Choose to Be the Master of Your Destiny

2.

Fix Your Mind on Specific Objectives

3.

Trim Your Expenses to Weigh Less Than Your Income

4.

Set Aside for Yourself a Part of Everything You Earn

5.

Increase Your Income by Multiplying Your Value to Others

6.

Invest With the Greatest Prudence and Safety

7.

Borrow Only What You Have the Ability to Repay

8.

Establish Good Habits and They Will Establish You

9.

Choose to Associate with Wise, Successful People

10.

Increase Your Wealth by Sharing It

Wealth and abundance are constantly lurking in the shadows of each person's life, ready to enter when invited in.

Chapter 1

THE FIRST LAW OF WEALTH AND ABUNDANCE

CHOOSE TO BE THE MASTER OF YOUR DESTINY!

Wealth and abundance constantly lurk in the shadows,
Ready to enter each person's life when invited in.

"Working, working, working, from dawn 'til dusk, and yet I get nowhere!"

Years ago this is how I described my life. I remember ruminating time and time again, "I shall never have enough to satisfy my desires and care for my family as is their due. It is clear that I am destined to live a life of poverty and want."

Little did I know then, as I do now, that any person can have a plentiful supply of money.

I was not aware at the time that there are ten simple laws which govern the accumulation of money and anyone can follow them if they put their minds to it.

As I recall, I had little else but a burning desire for the finer things in life: for my wife to be attired in the finest garments and to ride through the streets of Philadelphia in a horse-drawn carriage. For my sons, who were as yet a dream and a desire, to be well and thoroughly educated and to enjoy the best that life has to offer.

In those days I often said to myself, "Andrew Baldwin, you shall not always be a poor clerk! Someday you shall own your own shop and buildings and properties. You shall not always see your wife eat from wooden bowls with pewter spoons. No, man, some day your table will be set with fine English linens and china and silver spoons."

But did I really believe, with my heart and soul, that this dream would come true? Ah, no, the realities of my poverty constantly awakened me from my reverie. For in my younger days my father, mother, my eight sisters and brothers and I lived crowded together in two rooms. Although my father, a loyal and devoted man, always had gainful employment, there never seemed enough food to go around. My mother did what she could to help, making jams and jellies which we children peddled to shopkeepers. In fact, each of us, as soon as we were able, found work that would bring in money to help feed the family.

Later, after my beloved Rebecca and I married, we found it necessary to survive with the barest of necessities. Our one-room house was furnished with a bed and an old pine table and two chairs that had been discarded by another family and left on the street. On our wedding day, Rebecca's mother presented us with two tin plates, some knives and forks, two wooden bowls, and a pair of pewter mugs. Those things were the whole of our household possessions.

Yet from early on in my childhood, for some reason I shall never fully understand, I was never satisfied with my meager existence. I always knew, deep inside myself, that someday I would find a way to make things different. Something within me silently rejected the reality of poverty. I determined to fight against it.

However, I would hear my father's oft repeated observation, "Baldwins are destined to be poor." And then I heard his list of relatives, all experiencing poverty and want since coming to the New World. My father believed the Baldwins had always been poor, and thus, this sufficient evidence proved their lowly state was inevitable, a condition we would never be able to rise above.

In response, I felt guilty for daydreaming, and for not accepting the meager things we had. I dejectedly reminded myself, "Father is right. You are only Andrew Baldwin, the lad who wastes much time with daydreams, and will never be anything but a poor clerk. No one in your family has ever become anything more or acquired any kind of wealth. What makes you think you can? Give up these useless fantasies, for what is the point in building up hopes which will only be dashed?"

And so it went. My innermost desires and ambitions crushed by what I thought was unalterable reality.

Then on a warm summer afternoon in 1765, Providence smiled gently down on me. An event occurred that instilled within me a brighter hope for the future and started me on a thrilling road to prosperity. On that day a chance encounter with a total stranger changed my life forever.

I was one of a number of clerks working that day in our mercantile shop. We were busy and I barely heard the familiar tinkle of the bell above the door. Looking up, I saw a gentleman enter the store who tilted his head in courtesy to another patron. Several others in the shop seemed to know him, too, and treated him with great respect as he waited his turn at the counter. I found something oddly compelling about this gentleman and felt lucky I was free when it was his turn to be waited upon. I greeted him courteously, as I would have any other patron.

"Good afternoon, sir. How may I help you?"

"My good wife asked me to stop here and get this special blend of tea," he said as he extracted a slip of paper from his pocket.

"Earl Grey, it is," he informed me after looking at the note.

"Yes, of course, it is my pleasure to help you with this," I said. "Would you like the larger bag or a small one?"

"And which is the most economical?" he asked, eyeing me carefully.

"Your best value is the larger bag."

He nodded and told me that was what he wanted.

Although I suspected there was nothing else on his list, I inquired, as I would have with any customer, "Is there anything else you require today?"

"No, only the tea," he responded.

I nodded, but then added invitingly, "We have received a fresh shipment of Scottish shortbread that goes very nicely with afternoon tea. Many of our customers find that an unexpected gift of shortbread biscuits pleases their wives and guests very much." I said this as matter-of-factly as possible, for I sensed he was a man who did not respond well to arrogance or presumptuous behavior.

Indeed, he looked at me for a moment with no expression on his face, then he broke into a wide grin. He stepped closer to me and said, "Young man, I like you. I find your manner and initiative extremely refreshing. How could I resist such a courteous offer of a fine delicacy?"

"Thank you, sir."

As I wrapped the tea and biscuits and tallied the amount—seventeen pence—I took a good look at this gentleman. He was well dressed in a cut-away black broadcloth jacket, mustard-colored vest, and white shirt, though the appointments were not lavish. He appeared somewhat portly and walked with a cane, which I observed was necessary because of some trouble with his left foot. He wore his hair long beyond his balding pate, and wire-rimmed spectacles perched on his nose. Behind them his bright eyes sparkled with interest and pleasure in life.

I watched as he took out a worn leather purse, snapped open one compartment and carefully counted out the coins. I assumed from the care he took with his money that he, too, was a person who had to watch the coppers he spent.

I treated him as I would any other patron, as I have served hundreds of others in the years since I was fourteen and first began working in this shop. Yet there was something about this man that intrigued me. And it seemed that this old gentleman had also felt some spark lit between us, for as he was about to take his leave, he hesitated, then turned and looked at me. "Young man, might I again compliment you on your friendliness and initiative." He held up the package to indicate the biscuits.

"Thank you, sir," I replied.

"How long have you worked here, my young friend?"

"For six years. I began when I was fourteen, sir."

Again he smiled, then turned his head and looked at me from the corner of his eye and inquired, "And what are your ambitions, my young friend?"

"My ambitions?" I hesitated. "Sir, I am but a poor clerk. I aspire to gain much of course, but they are only dreams. I have no opportunity to make them realities."

He turned his head sharply back to face me and raised one finger. "Young man," he said with an emphatic tone. "Poverty is a state of mind. It is a choice a person makes."

He watched closely to see if comprehension lit up my face.

Instead, surely he saw only puzzlement there. "Poverty is a choice," I repeated his statement to myself. Everything within me and all my experience in life—my family and many of my friends and their fight to get by in their meager existence—gave mouth to the notion no one chooses a life of poverty. Why would anyone desire a life full of struggle and want? It did not make sense. Was this just an old man speaking in riddles? I yearned to challenge him.

Yet, I realized I must remember where I was standing, behind the counter of my employer's shop. It would be impertinent to argue with a customer. Instead, I replied, "Poverty is a choice? Sir, your words confound me. I am not at all sure I understand the point you are trying to make."

The gentleman leaned over the counter and asked in a low but firm voice, "Are you interested in improving your lot in life?"

"Of course," I answered. "Isn't everyone?"

Without responding, he examined me from close range, seeming to take in once again everything about my person. It appeared evident that little escaped his gaze. Finally he pulled back and spoke. "No, my friend, not everyone wants to improve his lot. Most people accept a life of poverty, never questioning the rightness or wrongness of it, never asking what they can do to change their places in life."

Once again, I struggled to understand how someone who seemed as prosperous and wise as this gentleman could espouse such an odd view of life. Again, I wanted to challenge him, yet I felt constrained by my situation from any confrontation with this seemingly wise man.

As luck would have it, at that moment the shop emptied of all other customers and the other clerks took the opportunity to retire to the back room. I examined, once again, the man before me, to try to gain some insight as to who he was and what he was telling me.

"Sir, why do you ask these questions? They are most unusual."

He smiled at me and chuckled. "Do you find these questions offensive, young man?"

"Oh no," I replied. "I find them exciting and challenging. No one has ever talked this way with me before."

"Am I being too personal? Or impertinent?" he inquired.

"Not at all sir."

"Then allow me to ask you this question once more: Are you interested in improving your lot in life?"

I wondered if he was only playing games with me, but I responded honestly. "Of course I am. I want to provide for my family and enjoy more of life's abundances."

Again he grinned and inspected me while rubbing his throat with his pudgy hand. He grimaced, shifting his weight to his right foot, leaned on his cane, and peered at me over the tiny glasses which sat perched halfway down his nose. Then, in a strong whisper, he said, "The way to wealth is as plain as the growth of a tree."

Once again I was puzzled by the things he said, although I felt sure if I listened and asked for more, all this information would begin to make sense.

What he said sounded so simple at first, but then reflecting for just a moment deeper layers of meaning revealed themselves.

I decided candor was the best way to proceed with this gentleman. "Forgive my ignorance, sir, but what you say makes little sense to me. A tree, if it gets the sun, water and soil that it needs will grow strong and straight. I do not see that it is this way with wealth and success."

"Thank you for your honesty," he replied. Then he repeated

what he had said, "The way to wealth is as plain as the growth of a tree!"

Once again he watched me, as if he wondered if I comprehended what he said to me. I am sure that my face flushed, for I did not want him to think my mind too simple.

He went on, "Poor people, my friend, are those who have failed to practice the laws which govern the accumulation of wealth. Like the things which cause the growth of a tree, the laws that govern the accumulation of money are simple."

"Simple, sir," I spoke before I thought. "Look about you at all the poor people who are struggling just to feed themselves. Why, look at me, I can barely provide for our rent and food! My life is committed to simply staying alive. I have not 'chosen' a life of poverty and I know of no 'simple' way to rise above it."

The gentleman chuckled. I could tell he immensely enjoyed my challenge. He looked at me squarely and spoke through a sly grin. "There are basic laws that govern prosperity, and the laws are few, my friend, and easily understood. To understand them, though, you must understand this truth: To be wealthy you must first choose to be the master of your destiny!"

Now the gentleman had my full attention and I listened eagerly as he continued. "You must take control of your life. You must make a decision to be wealthy. It must be uppermost among your desires."

I listened to his words, but I am afraid I still missed his full meaning. Torn between admitting my lack of understanding and pretending that I comprehended, I realized my pretense would hardly escape his attention. I responded, "Sir, I disagree. Most people have no control over what they do with their lives! Most work hard just to survive. They have no way to rise above their meager conditions."

"Oh, I agree," he retorted with swiftness. "Most people move through life so overcome with thoughts of survival they never take hold of their lives and achieve the wealth which awaits them. But most could do so, if they wanted to, and if they knew how," he said, carefully emphasizing his last point. "Wealth and abundance are forever lurking in the shadows of each person's life, ready to enter when invited in."

"Invited in?" I responded.

"Yes," he replied.

"But sir," I protested, "there are many of us who, without family inheritances, have no hope of enjoying anything but a meager existence."

The gentleman lowered his gaze to his fine leather shoes then shook his head slowly. "You are wrong, my young friend. People who think this make a choice for poverty. They either choose to be poor or they choose abundance! Everyone makes choices that then become the seedlings of their future."

Again his eyes challenged me, as if to ascertain my understanding.

"But sir, no one would will to be poor!"

"Perhaps not directly, my young friend. But people choose poverty by their inaction. They choose it by not taking the trouble to overcome their ignorance. They choose it by not fighting back." He punched the air to emphasize his point.

"Another way people choose poverty is by accepting as fact the mistaken notion that they must play out their lives as others expect them. They accept poverty when they fail to stand up and say to themselves and to the world, 'I can choose my destiny! I can chart my own course! I can rise above imposed limitations!' Family advantages or disadvantages should not determine anyone's destiny. Nor should the expectations of others. Nor external conditions. Poverty is a choice and our choices become the seedlings of our future realities," he repeated.

He thought a moment, staring out the store window, again slowly rubbing his throat with his pudgy hand. "What do you get when you plant a grain of corn?"

His question seemed too simple, so I hesitated a moment in answering. As he waited for my response, I felt his gaze penetrating my mind so I was honest about my confusion. "What do you get, sir?"

"Yes."

"Well, I suppose you get a corn stalk."

"Exactly. And if you plant an apple seed what do you get?"

"An apple tree," I responded.

"You are correct, my young friend. You see, in nature seeds always reproduce their own kind in multiplied quantities. Plant a seed of corn and you get ears with many more seeds. Plant an apple seed and nature yields a tree full with apples containing many seeds in them. Seeds always yield their own kind in multiplied quantities. So it is with your seeds of thought and action. Choose to plant the seeds of expectations of abundance and eventually your thoughts will yield those fruits in multiplied quantities."

Within the blink of an eye, I began to get insight into what he was saying to me.

"And might I ask you another question?" he asked.

"Of course, sir."

Once again I became the victim of his intense gaze. As he studied my face he asked, "And who controls your choices in life? Who controls your thoughts and actions?"

For a moment I was stunned at the directness of his question. The best answer was obvious: I, myself, controlled the choices I made about my life. Yet there was still some part of me that hesitated to voice this conviction. Once again an image of my father's face and his plight in life rose before me, reminding me that the Baldwins had always been poor labourers.

But his pressing me was not over. "And how will you begin controlling your choices?" he asked in a quiet, yet most direct manner.

I knew I needed to reflect on the simple question before I answered it. Once again, I wondered, "Who is this person? Is he just an old man who loves to hear himself give advice? Or is he someone who truly knows of what he speaks?"

"Sir, this advice you give," I softly but pointedly asked aloud, "do you practice it yourself?"

For a moment he looked me squarely in the eye, then he laughed heartily and slapped his knee. As I walked from behind the counter he reached around and tapped my foot lightly with his cane, winked at me, and chuckled. "Good question! Good question! You have me there! To be honest, the answer is yes...and no! Yes, I do practice my own advice. No, I do not do so as much as some think I should!"

Pausing for a moment, he went on, "At age twelve I entered the apprenticeship of my brother. I learned a trade from him. When, with a stubborn will, I refused to accept his limiting beliefs about me, he attempted to break me and prevent my ambition from expressing itself. So I left his print shop in Boston and came to Philadelphia when I was seventeen. Then I sailed to England when I was eighteen. Returning to Philadelphia a year later, I made a firm resolve to be the master of my own destiny. I began to plan my future. I saw my fortune in publishing, yet I was severely criticized by those close to me."

I wanted to believe his story, yet wondered if he had really done these things.

"Criticized?" I asked aloud. "For what?"

"Well, there were already three or four printing shops in the colonies. People warned me that I had selected a trade which was already overpopulated. However, I dreamed of publishing newspapers, books and almanacs and I was ready to act on my beliefs. I exercised my power of choice and made a firm decision. I chose to shape my future with my own hands, and to take action in the belief I could reach any goal I set out to achieve."

He paused and looked at me with his piercing eyes. Then he said with an emphatic tone, "If you truly choose to be the master of your destiny, then you have obeyed the first law of wealth and abundance!"

With a countenance of quietness, yet power, he searched my face for a moment, then extended a hand to me before he turned to leave. I watched him approach the door, which opened before he got there, admitting a lady customer. The gentleman tipped his hat as he stepped aside to let her pass.

She looked up at him and exclaimed, "Mr. Franklin! How nice to see you this afternoon!"

"Mr. Franklin!" I gasped as the realization stuck me. "I have been talking to the great Ben Franklin!"

I rushed to the door, then followed the gentleman as he stepped into the street. "Are you *the* Mr. Franklin?" I asked, suddenly aghast that I had been so forward with him. "The *famous* Ben Franklin?"

"I am Ben Franklin," he responded, "but 'famous,' well, that's a question that could cause some heated debate in some circles," he smiled.

Imagine me, Andrew Baldwin, the clerk, talking to the great

Ben Franklin! I thought my heart would leap to my throat.

At that moment I learned a tremendous lesson: Great men are usually quite willing to share their knowledge and wisdom with those younger and less fortunate. I learned, too, that wise men will gladly spend time with those who sincerely desire to learn from them.

"Mr. Franklin," I spoke, with an unsure voice.

"Yes, my friend"

"Well...sir...I...well, I know you are a person of much renown in our city, as in the world. And I know you have traveled the world over and your influence extends across oceans. And people revere you for your charities and public service."

He again smiled modestly, helping confidence to rise within me, so I continued.

"And is it not true, sir, that you started out in life the same as me, a poor boy with little in the way of family advantages? Is that not correct, sir?"

"Yes, yes. In fact my first employment came as a soap boiler's helper."

"A soap boiler?"

"Yes," he chuckled. "And my nostrils still carry the unpleasant memories, although many decades now separate us. My humble beginnings are a fact of life of which I have often reminded myself when I slip into the habit of taking myself a bit too seriously."

"Sir, I am embarrassed that I have wasted your time with my poor manners," I said, thinking this might be my only chance to talk to him and not wanting to ruin it. "I had no knowledge of who you are."

"Feel no need to apologize, my young friend. This conversation has not been a waste of my time. We will meet again. Until we do meet again, though, remember the first law of wealth and abundance: *Choose to be the master of your destiny!"*

He paused a moment, searching me, before he broke eye contact, then turned, and waddled down the cobblestone walk, his cane tapping the stones, smiling and waving to passersby.

The First Law of Wealth and Abundance

CHOOSE TO BE THE MASTER OF YOUR DESTINY!

Choose abundance, not poverty. Plant thought-seeds of prosperity, not pauperism, with your choices and actions. Commit to learn the laws which govern the accumulation of wealth. Accept responsibility for your own individual successes. Stop blaming circumstances, conditions, or other people. Agree to pay the price of learning and effort. Resolve not to allow temporary defeat to be accepted as failure. Be willing to prudently take risks. Ask for guidance from your Creator and those who have demonstrated by their actions that they are wise in the ways of success. Spend time with those who have chosen prosperity and abundance. Understand their patterns of thought and action.

Chapter 2

THE SECOND LAW OF WEALTH AND ABUNDANCE

FIX YOUR MIND ON SPECIFIC OBJECTIVES

Decide in your mind exactly what you desire.
Continually think about it and it will ultimately transpire!

For days I could think of little more than my conversation with this great man. Could I, as he suggested, really be the master of my destiny? Could I rise above my current level of poverty? Truly, are there laws that, when followed with dedication, can lead to wealth and abundance?

My mind spun with these and many other unanswered questions, and I waited with anxiousness for Mr. Franklin to visit the store again.

Each time I heard the bells chime upon the opening of the door, my head popped up, hoping I would see him entering. I calculated innumerable times the days it would take his wife to use up the tea I sold him, praying he would then come back for more.

I questioned anyone who knew him for clues about his daily habits. Did he often welcome people into his home? Several people told me yes, which in my mind meant that the tea was being served to their numerous guests and used up with alacrity and that Mr. Franklin would be needing more soon.

Of course, I had recounted to my bride, Rebecca, every word of my momentous conversation with this great man. She exhibited the same excitement and intrigue which I felt and joined me in anticipation for our next encounter.

Yet, she also made a wise and important suggestion not to wait for Mr. Franklin to further explain his philosophy, but to remind myself every day of his words: "I choose to be the master of my destiny!"

I responded to her suggestion with enthusiasm, and each day upon arising stated those wise words. I then repeated the phrase, less vociferously, whenever reminded throughout the day. I chanted it as I walked to my place of employment. I whispered it at the end of each transaction I made at the store. I said it after my blessing before I ate my lunch. And I repeated it loudly and with conviction from within the embrace with which I greeted Rebecca upon returning home at the end of the day.

I did all this without knowing exactly how or what the result would be. But I soon discovered that the daily affirmations began to cause changes in me. I found myself searching for answers to this riddle. I developed a greater desire to have more than I had. With a slow dawning, I felt a sense of dissatisfaction with the poverty that had previously filled my mind.

I began to entertain the possibility of enjoying more of this world's goods. A feeling of strong desire commenced to take hold of me. All because of a chance meeting with this great man and his enthusiastic adherence to the basic principle of his philosophy of success.

I realized that although I did not at that time fully understand the impact or importance of this meeting and this philosophy to my life, I knew for certain that Providence had smiled with gentle favor upon me.

My waiting proved fruitful a fortnight after our first encounter when Mr. Franklin once again walked into the store. Luck being with me, the store was empty and I was the sole clerk working at the counter.

As always, my head snapped up when I heard the door bells chime.

Much to my elation, Mr. Franklin greeted me warmly. He stated that upon walking by the store he thought to enter and inquire about the progress of my battle with destiny. He further asserted that no; he did not need anything, but thought a few moments of my company would be most enjoyable.

Mr. Franklin was the best-known person in the colonies, for his *Poor Richard's Almanack* had given him wide renown. However, I discovered during conversation regarding his habits and schedule, that his philanthropic accomplishments and his inventions and discoveries were just as numerous and significant.

He established the first public library in 1731. In 1736, he organized the first fire company, including both a paid and a volunteer corps of fire watchmen in the Union Fire Company. He formed the American Philosophical Society in 1743. His benevolence led him to establish the Pennsylvania Hospital in 1751. In 1752, he formed the first successful fire insurance company.

His genius and industry had resulted in a plenitude of helpful inventions, such as the Franklin Stove, lightning rods to prevent homes from catching fire, and vents for street lamps to keep the soot from building up in the glass.

"How were you able to achieve all these great successes?" I asked that afternoon.

He smiled at me, his keen eyes peering over his glasses, rubbed his throat with his pudgy hand, and replied, "My young friend, we are given, by the Almighty, twenty-four hours in a day. This is a resource we all share and in that sense we are equal. My observation is that people handle their time in different manners. Some spend their time thinking only of survival. They concern themselves with accumulating enough money to buy food to eat and to pay for their other necessities such as rent and clothing. Their minds dwell on little else, so they achieve only what they set their minds to achieve, which is bare survival.

"There are still others who fix their minds on pleasure. To them, work is only necessary as it provides them with the funds they need to enjoy their individual dalliances. The ale houses are filled with these types of people. They get what they set their minds to achieve. I, and others like me who have achieved certain loftier goals in their lives, look beyond these levels. We fix our minds on higher attainments."

"Pardon me for interrupting, sir, but could you be more specific? Tell me how you do that."

Mr. Franklin looked at me and smiled. I had hoped that in my questions he saw the fire of ambition and a strong desire to learn and know—both qualities I knew he admired and valued.

"I'm delighted your mind did not allow my point to escape its attention," he smiled. "To fix your mind on certain objectives is to decide exactly what you desire. One of my first desires was, through industry and frugality, to attain a level of financial independence. I fixed within me an aim to retire before I was fifty years old, and to direct my efforts at philanthropy. I wanted to do whatever I could to make our city, as well as our world, a better place in which to live. This became an important force, driving me to succeed.

"At first my good wife and I were willing to live with sparseness and frugality in order to some day enjoy our desired financial independence. I might add that I achieved that plan for my life well ahead of time."

I was amazed that he could do that, and asked, "You mean you were actually able to retire before you were fifty years old?" This was a new idea to me. Obsessed with the status quo, I assumed I would work until the day my body was carried off to the potter's field. "You actually stopped working and still possess enough money to live on? That just does not seem possible!"

"Indeed, I assure you it did happen. In order to do all this I learned early a basic principle."

He paused as if to emphasize the import of what he would next say. "The principle is simply that he who aims to thrive, must ask his wife!"

I still picture today the small, thin-rimmed spectacles propped on his nose below his receding hairline. I was always captivated by the way his soft hazel eyes danced with merriment, as if he were anticipating my reaction to this advice. Caught off guard, expecting lofty words of ancient wisdom, I at first could do nothing but stand thinking. Then his words sparked a sudden understanding within me.

"I understand your point, sir," I said. "I, like you, am blessed with a good wife who makes no extravagant demands on our funds and is supportive of my dreams and desires. In fact, she already feels as if she knows you, for I have recounted to her the many details of our last meeting."

"Then you are fortunate, my friend, to have such an understanding soul for a wife."

"Tell me sir," I went on. "Please give me another example of how you fixed your mind on specific ambitions. I am curious to know."

He seemed to contemplate for a moment and said, "Well, there have been many times. For instance, early in my years I became fascinated with the powers of electricity and how it could be harnessed. So I fixed in my mind the desire to understand it and capture it.

"For long periods of time I thought of little else. I ran all kinds of experiments—some quite foolish—I might add. No one will ever believe this, and it certainly will not be remembered in history as being of any significance, but one of my experiments concerned the observation of electricity in lightning bolts. I actually flew a kite in a severe thunderstorm."

He roared with laughter and slapped his knee with his hand. "Well, I almost got myself killed, but I made a great discovery. I tied a metal key on the kite string to see if the string would conduct electricity when the lightning hit.

"There I stood in a thunderstorm until a lightning bolt cracked open the sky, hit the kite, sent an electrical charge down through the string, lit the key like a candle, and knocked me to the ground! Curiosity nearly got the best of me, but I found out what I wanted to know!"

We both laughed soundly for a moment at the image of Mr. Franklin flying a kite in a thunderstorm. Then he looked me squarely in the face as if to ensure that I did not miss his next point.

"We always procure what we want most to have, regardless of our beginnings. We accomplish what we fix our minds on getting! Now, you, my young friend Andrew, what is it you want most to possess in your life?"

The suddenness and directness of his question caught me off guard. "Well," I fumbled, "I suppose I want to provide my family with more luxuries and conveniences...and...some day to own land

and buildings and property...and...like you, sir, to make the world a better place in which to live."

"If these are your true desires," he said, "you can have them. But they must be your compelling passion, you must think of them morning, noon and night. You must fix in your mind your specific desires for wealth not in a general sense, but you must be precise as if aiming for a target."

In the days following this conversation, I thought much of what Mr. Franklin had said. I knew he was right, yet many doubts filled my mind. "Sure," I argued with myself, "anyone can give advice like that and maybe because of his great intelligence, he can reach ambitions that he wants to reach. But I am only a poor clerk. There are thousands of other people, just like me, who will live and die and make no impact upon the world."

Once again Rebecca encouraged me. "Why don't we do as he advises? Why don't we set some specific goals?"

Gradually realizing my resistance had only to do with my fear of failing, I resolved to press on. I realized I had little to lose and much to gain by trying, and if I failed I would be in no different position than I was at that time.

So, I set about defining specific ambitions, which I soon discovered to not be a simple task.

With the task of setting ambitions I learned an important lesson about human nature: The reason many people do not desire specific aspirations is because they do not believe it is possible to be any different than they now are. They do not take the time and discipline to fix in their minds exactly what they want to achieve, because it is so comfortable to remain as they are. But, on a deeper level, I have observed that many people do not feel worthy of enjoying the finer things of life. They are quite settled in with their low estates.

For several days I considered the principle Franklin had taught me. I spent days thinking about what my specific ideals would be. Then I entered them in a little booklet, analyzed them and, of course, discussed them with Rebecca. As I now recall, I set these objectives:

1. To increase my earnings as a clerk twenty percent in one year. To achieve this I pledged to analyze my work habits and implement one new improvement each week, soon putting me in a position to earn more.
2. To learn from my employer the art and skill of account keeping, so that within one year I could take over that duty.
3. To purchase new kitchen items for our home.
4. To purchase for Rebecca, in appreciation for her support, materials for two new dresses.

As I look back at these desires, they seem so very modest now, but at the time they appeared like the tallest mountains to climb. However, the moment I committed them to writing I felt like a different person. All at once, I had more energy and strength and I found my work taking on a new meaning. The days passed quickly, consumed as I was with accomplishing my ambitions. I worked with much joy each day, storing up accomplishments, looking forward to the end of the day when I could triumphantly report them to Rebecca.

My employer, Mr. Whitworth, was immediately impressed with my enthusiasm and acknowledged it with complimentary comments. This gave me the courage to approach him about learning the account-keeping practices. One day I asked, "Sir, could I ask for a few moments of your time?"

"Of course," was his reply, and he pointed to two empty barrels in the storeroom. "Take a seat."

"Sir, you are a very successful person of business," I began.

"Thank you, Andrew."

"I want very much to improve my situation in life and have been wondering...well...would you teach me more about what makes a business such as yours operate successfully?"

"And what is it you want to learn?"

"Sir, I want to learn account-keeping. I want to learn from your experiences. I appreciate the job you have given me, and I do enjoy my work as a clerk, but...well...I do not want to remain in that position all my life. I want to advance myself. I want to provide more for Rebecca and the children we hope to have. I want her to have better clothes. I want to provide her with servants, to have a larger home, to entertain friends..."

He smiled at me and nodded as he told me he understood my desires, he was impressed with my intentions and my desire to learn, and he would be happy to work with me. Then he invited me into the room where he kept all the store's records.

There he explained to me, "Andrew, this is where much of the success of our business is controlled. Yes, if we do not have merchandise our patrons want at prices they will pay we will not have sales, and if we do not have sales we do not have anything to write in these books. However, it is these records that help me manage the business effectively and determine what it is the patrons want and what they will pay for it.

"Andrew," he went on, "I have sensed in you the desirable trait of industry and initiative. I like that. If you are truly interested in learning account-keeping, I will gladly teach you. You can also help me with posting entries into the journals and ledgers. This way," he explained, "by actually doing the work, you will learn faster."

We agreed beginning that very day, he would spend one hour, after closing, teaching me the skills of account-keeping.

During the next few weeks he explained all his records and the different journals and ledgers, his cash receipts and disbursements. He gave me an inside look at how his business functioned.

I learned about all our expenses and the costs of merchandise. He explained the necessity of profits, as well as how they can be diminished by inadequate or careless management. Eventually together we began to set sales and profit objectives. We also set plans for such things as monthly merchandise turnover and percentage of costs against sales.

During this time Mr. Whitworth often told me, "Andrew, because you are such a good apprentice, I find myself being a better manager. You are not the only one who is learning from this."

We became close together during those months of tutelage, and Mr. Whitworth came to trust me more and more. From this small beginning, I learned much about the power of specific ambitions.

Once I set a desire to increase my earnings twenty percent within a year, I began to ask myself, "How can I become more productive so Mr. Whitworth can afford to reward me more?"

At first, answers to this question came to me quite slowly. I suppose part of me held on to my old beliefs that I could not improve my lot. But because I continued to ask I began to discover answers.

Sparingly at first, I saw solutions where I had not seen them before. For instance, I distributed notes to our more affluent customers, Mr. Franklin included, offering a delivery service. I suggested that if they had their servants bring a list of their requirements to the store we would select the items and deliver them within the day.

Within a very brief time, our business enjoyed a significant increase because of this service. I assumed the responsibility of hiring young boys to make the deliveries. With each shipment I included a short note to our customers thanking them and asking them to remember us to their friends and neighbors. In time this brought in much new business.

Delighted with the success of this new service, Mr. Whitworth increased my weekly pay. I was struck with the reality that my additional pay was just over the twenty percent increase I had targeted. A coincidence? If it was, I was to soon experience many other such coincidences as a result of my setting high standards for myself.

Rebecca and I began to allow ourselves to dream about what we could have in life. I took her to see a furniture maker about building a few pieces for our house, and we looked at beautiful fabrics from which she could make her well-deserved dresses. We began to look at larger homes, even though at that time we could not afford them.

At first we felt guilty looking at things we could not afford, but soon we became accustomed to it, and we agreed it was exciting and gave us much to laugh and dream about. It was here that I first understood that dreams are indeed the seedlings of realities.

I began to gain a glimpse of what I would one day discover as the secret of all achievement.

I prepared a small board which I hung over my work desk. The sign bore a slogan that helped me acquire much of what I now have. Its wisdom has proven true many times in the ensuing years, suggesting a truth that will bring almost anything into a person's life if he or she sincerely wants to possess it. This is how the statement read:

Decide in your mind exactly what you desire.

Continually think about it and it will ultimately transpire.

Each day I read this statement numerous times. Each day I attempted to gain a new insight into the truth it contained. At first I understood it only on a very elementary level, as it applied to specific financial goals I had set. Then I began to understand this great law on more profound dimensions, as it applied to my values and even my physical health. As time and experiences advanced, I came to understand that there are two distinctly different functions of my mind. One is the conscious part that I use for everyday decisions and to learn facts and information. This part of my mind helps me think through problems and other logical processes.

But in time I discovered a vast and more powerful creative force within me, a force that went to work for me the moment I fixed my mind on desirable aspirations, as I began to believe them possible for me to achieve, and as I felt worthy to receive them.

I soon discovered that at night I had sudden flashes of insight and, upon awakening, forthrightly found solutions to problems with which I had previously been wrestling. This creative part of me gradually began to reveal ways to reach the aspirations to which I had committed.

It seemed this part of me did not sleep, but while my body was resting, processed ways I could reach my goals. I became intrigued with this powerful and mysterious part of me that gave me hunches and flashes of insight. Finally, during one of our weekly visits, I asked Mr. Franklin about it.

"My young friend," he replied with a fatherly smile, "your question indicates you are indeed growing in wisdom and understanding." He chuckled again and looking soberly at me replied, "My student is indeed learning." By his slight grin, I could tell he was pleased with my progress.

"And how do you plan to use this new-found knowledge?" he asked, without really answering my question.

Fumbling for a reply, I finally said, "Sir, it was…it was my hope that you would tell me how I can use this knowledge. Do you experience these same sensations? Are you often awakened or surprised with answers to your own questions?"

That day Mr. Franklin helped me understand more fully the source of all success and accomplishment. He confirmed that there are indeed two parts of each person's mind—the conscious and the unconscious.

"Most people use only the more easily accessible part—the conscious," he said. "Few people take the trouble to discover the creative unconscious part. Most people are so focused on their own survival and their everyday problems that they never find themselves in a position to discover this inner creative power."

He then went on to explain that all his discoveries came as a result of turning problems over to this powerful unconscious and then allowing it to come up with solutions.

He finally pulled his metal-rimmed spectacles from his nose.

"Here," he said, holding them up for me to see. "Take these glasses, for example. Let me tell you how my mind gave me the idea for them. As you will discover when you are older, glasses which are proper for reading are not best for greater distances. It becomes necessary to have two pairs of glasses, which is inconvenient for obvious reasons. From the moment this problem struck me, I began to look for a solution; for days it was my passion and my obsession. I examined possibilities in ways of carrying and storing two pairs of glasses and ways of wearing two pairs of glasses at once. Unable to find an answer that satisfied me, for a while I dismissed the idea in frustration. Then early one morn several days later I awakened with an image flashing into my mind of a lens ground on top for distance and on the bottom for reading. My unconscious mind had been working on the problem despite the fact that my conscious mind had dismissed it and moved on to everyday problems.

"I call them bifocals. They are only a temporary measure, to be sure, but they work for me now. Undoubtedly, someone will perfect a better idea soon."

He paused in reflection, then said, "Every idea or invention I have ever discovered has come to me in the same manner."

I felt a rush of excitement swell from within me; as if a whole new discovery had been made, as indeed it had. For days it overtook my thoughts. Each day I became more and more excited about the possibilities for my own achievement.

Learning that Mr. Franklin was also fascinated by this great inner power resource, I felt challenged and inspired to explore its powers more fully for myself.

At first I vowed to use this hidden power in my pursuit of wealth, but as time went by, and my needs changed, I began to apply this concept in every part of my life.

I continued to formulate and write down objectives for my business, determining where I wanted to be at specific points in the future. Then I also wrote the personal qualities I needed to form my habits. I consulted Rebecca and together we listed our hopes for trips, special occasions and times spent together. I developed the habit of reading these desires daily and picturing myself having already attained them. I sought the help of the Almighty through prayer. I learned through experience that He answers me with moments of insight and intuition.

All this helped me gain access to the powerful unconscious part of my mind—the part that lies within everyone just waiting to be discovered and used. I soon learned to delegate responsibility for solving problems and generating new ideas to this hidden part of me. I began to trust it with matters of decision, and I grew stronger and stronger in my ability to hear its voice.

This habit would, in time, be my main resource for gaining the vast wealth I eventually attained.

But I am moving ahead of the chronology of my story, so allow me to go back and share what I began to learn. Then in the remaining chapters I will take you step-by-step through the depths to which the knowledge of this great power ultimately progressed.

Again, I remind you that having a surplus of money doesn't lie only in knowing the laws I share with you. True abundance is the effect of certain deeper causes that I will share with you throughout this book.

Yes, it all began with a simple slogan I repeated to myself over and over. It then led me to discover the way to unlimited prosperity and abundance, as well as helping me enjoy the better things in life. The simple slogan, again, is:

Decide in your mind exactly what you desire.

Continually think about it and it will ultimately transpire!

The Second Law of Wealth and Abundance

FIX YOUR MIND ON SPECIFIC OBJECTIVES

Decide exactly what you want to achieve. Write down specific things that you want to have, gain, possess or enjoy. Set these objectives in several areas of your life – financial, personal, family and spiritual. Describe the exact amount of money you want to have at specific points in the future. Describe habits or attitudes or spiritual qualities you wish to possess. Define specific job, business or career ambitions. Write down strengths you will need to achieve these aspirations. Commit to daily activities that will lead you to your aspirations. Set goals to grow in wisdom and spiritual discernment. Learn to discover and access your powerful unconscious thoughts to give you guidance in reaching your aspirations. Then listen to your hunches and intuition as guides for your journey. Most importantly, take action on the insights that will be presented to you.

Chapter 3

The Third Law of Wealth and Abundance

TRIM YOUR EXPENSES TO WEIGH LESS THAN YOUR INCOME

Wise men do their incomes know,
And where all their expenses go!

At first, as I set and then achieved my desire to earn more money, I laboured under the false assumption that if I earned more, I would have more.

Unhappily, I had to learn the hard way that this is a common misconception, and that an important principle to understand and conquer is that, "Our spending mysteriously increases so as to devour all of our available income."

It all began after Mr. Whitworth, a thrifty man of Scottish descent, began tutoring me in account-keeping and increasing my knowledge of good store management. A few months later he said to me, "Andrew, your inquiring mind has indeed learned quickly. Your efforts have helped free up some of my own time. Because of the other responsibilities you have assumed, particularly that of managing all our other clerks and instituting and managing the delivery service which has been so successful, I have decided to expand the business."

I was, of course, delighted to hear that, and I expressed my excitement to him.

I have looked back on this event many times, although I couldn't fully understand its full significance then. I later saw it as one of the great developments in my business life, a turning point. But more importantly—it taught me an early lesson about the value of initiative and the "extra mile" philosophy that I was beginning to learn from my mentor, the great Benjamin Franklin.

Now, I return to my story. Mr. Whitworth continued, "I have made arrangements to purchase the building adjoining to the east of us in order to double the size of our space. As a result, I am giving you even more responsibility. Not only will you oversee the activities of the other clerks and the delivery service, but you will also help me purchase goods for our inventory.

"I am also giving you an increase in pay," Mr. Whitworth continued, "which I must say you have earned with your industry and initiative."

"An increase in pay? Oh, thank you, sir," I interrupted with great enthusiasm, but he waved me off.

"I will also pay you extra amounts every three months, based on our profits," he took time to explain with more specific information. "You are discovering a law that will serve you well, Andrew," he wisely advised, "and that is as you help create wealth for others, they will gladly share it with you."

I rushed home that evening, filled with enthusiasm. Opening the door, I announced my good news to Rebecca. We decided to celebrate. We gathered our money, went to the Bluebird Inn and indulged in the first dinner we had ever eaten away from our home. During dinner we talked about how we would use the extra funds. We discussed getting some new pieces of furniture we had dreamed of owning. That evening Rebecca told me we would, in a few months, have a new arrival. I shouted with joy and announced it to everyone in the dining room.

We immediately began to lay plans for our new child. We would need more room, a cradle for the baby, clothing...

"It will cost so much money!" Rebecca said.

"But we can afford it now that I am earning more."

"We can?" she responded. "Are you sure?"

Brimming with confidence, I assured her we could. "With my increased income, there are several things that we can now afford."

We smiled at each other, so happy with our new prosperity and success. We spent the whole evening talking about all the items we could now acquire. Our whole world seemed to be changing.

Well, by the time Benjamin was born, I had increased my income quite substantially. It almost doubled the previous year's amount because of the quarterly profit sharing that Mr. Whitworth gave me.

But to my surprise and sorrow, I discovered, although I had substantially exceeded my income goals, I had ended the year as void of savings as when I began it. We did have more luxuries, at the end of a year of increased income, but we still had no surplus of funds.

I was baffled! "Where did all the money go?" I asked myself. It did not seem we had spent all that much more. We only bought a few items, and those were certainly not extravagant. We thought they were most necessary.

"This cannot be right!" I said, denying to myself our circumstances. "We could not have spent all of my increased income!"

I began a quick investigation into why I had not ended the year with extra funds. I discovered that, try as I might, I could find only a few tangible things to show for my money. I was not only shocked,

I was angry with myself for not being able to explain what had happened to my increased income.

As I examined my spending habits during the previous few months I realized just how much we had spent on items we did not need or that were quickly consumed by our increased appetites.

It was around this time Mr. Franklin stopped by the shop, as he had often done. As always I felt, when I first saw him, some unworthiness that a man of his stature might be wasting his time on me. However, this concern was quickly neutralized by his warmth and the sincere interest he showed me. I realized once again that he had the ability to cause me to see the best in myself, as many great people do.

"And how are your fortunes going, Mr. Baldwin?" came his cheerful voice on the heels of the front door's ringing bell.

All I could respond to his greeting was, "Oh, Mr. Franklin."

"You're looking well, my friend, but a bit down in the mind," he observed as his cane tap, tap, tapped across the plank floors of the shop. "How are your fortunes going?" he repeated as he reached the counter.

"My fortunes? Well sir, not so well...not so well I am afraid."

"Oh. You sound as if you would rather not discuss the subject. What is the source of your discouragement?"

I never felt fully prepared for his perceptiveness, his uncanny ability to read my feelings. It was as if I were a window glass and he possessed the ability to look right through me. I had, of course, shared my successes with him during the past year. He knew how I had taken on much of the account-keeping responsibilities, how I was managing the other clerks in the store, and how the delivery service had proved to be such a profitable venture. He also remembered how Mr. Whitworth had rewarded me so handsomely. I proudly told him I had met and exceeded my income goals. He seemed genuinely excited for me and proud of me, as if I were his protégé. It would now be so hard to share with him my distress over our failed savings, yet I could not keep these problems from him. "Source of my discouragement, sir?" I stalled, nevertheless.

"Yes," he said, swinging his arms and almost hitting some sacks of cornmeal with his cane. "You look as dejected as a cat who has been told that there are no more mice in town."

"Forgive me," was all I could reply.

"And why have you chosen to feel badly?" He tilted his head and looked at me closely, emphasizing the word "chosen."

"I am angry with and disappointed in myself," I replied with some exasperation, finally giving in to my desire to discuss my troubles with this man despite what he might think of me. "One year ago I resolved to turn my fortunes around by increasing my income by twenty percent, thereby elevating myself from the demeaning state of poverty I was in. As you advised, I was intent on achievement."

"And you did, my young friend!" Mr. Franklin crowed with delight and pride.

Without the enthusiasm that Mr. Franklin had displayed, I said, "Oh, yes, and not only that but I almost doubled my income, far exceeding my goal."

"That is indeed commendable, young Andrew. So what is the problem that causes you so much alarm today?"

"The problem, sir, is although I earned more money because of my increased productivity and responsibility, I have no more surplus today than I did one year ago! Not only that," I went on, embarrassed, looking down at my feet as I spoke, "but I seem to have accumulated even more debt."

"Well," he said with a smile, "do let us talk about this strange happening."

Motioning to two boxes, he invited me to sit down. "My boy, do you have something I can rest my foot on?"

I slid a small box over and he lowered his left foot onto the box, sighing with relief. Grimacing, he said, "Remember young man, pride and gout are seldom cured throughout." Saying this he chuckled, as if to offer a slight apology for his rhyme.

After getting settled, Mr. Franklin turned to me. "Now, where did all your increased earnings go, my young friend?"

"That is just it, sir; I have not the slightest idea. I do not seem to have increased my expenditures that much. We had a child, as you know, so we had to purchase a cradle and a few other things. Rebecca and her mother made most of his clothing, so there was not much extra expense in that. We did rent a larger home, for our one room was not large enough, as we needed more room for the baby. So now we have a small but fine home with three rooms.

"And it appears, upon further investigation," I added, "that our appetites have unknowingly expanded with more expensive food and luxuries for our home. Often I have demonstrated my love for Rebecca by purchasing new clothes and other gifts for her."

Hearing this Mr. Franklin grinned knowingly. "We are taxed twice for our appetites," he remarked.

"Yes sir, I have discovered that," I replied.

"Well," Franklin sighed. "Savings and convenience seldom travel the same road together. Our spending can mysteriously increase so as to devour all our available income.

"I'm certain that you haven't just been waiting for me to bore you with maxims, but I must probe further. Tell me, young friend, tell me again what you have now that you did not have at this time last year."

"Well, as I said, our son, Benjamin was born." Mention of Benjamin's name seemed to distract Mr. Franklin for a moment.

I watched a flush creep over his face, remembering the honor we wanted to bestow on him by naming our firstborn after him. I hope it pleased him.

As busy and influential as he was, he, upon hearing of the birth of Benjamin, deposited ten gold crowns in a banking institution with careful instructions that it not be drawn out until our son was twenty-one years old.

The man was indeed a marvel. He even calculated how much those ten crowns would be worth at six percent compounded interest. Added to this he clearly informed us that the money could only be used for education, otherwise it would revert to the Pennsylvania Hospital, which he helped found in 1751.

"I am sorry!" Mr. Franklin said, causing me to come back to this place and time. "What were you saying?"

"I was speaking of my extra expenditures," I reminded him. "There were the things for Benjamin and then a few other items."

"Oh, yes," he smiled, peering through his round coin-sized bifocal spectacles, rubbing his throat as he thought. He eyed me for a moment and then went on, "A few coppers here, a few pence there, and, before you know it, your extra shillings of income have been silently eaten by your newly created appetites. This is a common mistake."

His manner told me to accept the responsibility of my actions while understanding the banality of them.

"Many people fall prey to this trap," he went on, "and it is one, if you truly desire to be wealthy, you must earnestly avoid."

Then with a twinkle in his eyes, he recited this little rhyme:

"Wise men do their incomes know,
And where all their expenses go!"

He chuckled as if he was poking a bit of fun at himself, but immediately he turned serious. "I know of no wealthy people who prove exceptions to this law." Having said this, he looked squarely at me, giving me time to allow his wisdom to lodge in my mind.

He then offered some other helpful suggestions about handling money and how I could correct the source of my problem. The plan he presented was a foolproof way to make sure my monthly expenses would no longer get out of hand.

At his urging, I procured a small account book from a stationery store. On the first page I carefully listed all the debts I owed. I found once I had summoned the courage to do this I immediately felt much better.

Then I wrote a letter to each lender acknowledging the debt and assuring them that the money would be paid in time. I did some calculations and discovered with ten percent of my income paid each month to these creditors, I could have the debts all paid off within one year. I gained much assurance and confidence from this calculation. It was such a simple discovery, but it profoundly taught me a great lesson.

Next, I ruled off space in the memorandum book for each month. At the top of each page I entered my income. I then divided the monthly spaces into these sections:

Debts
Fixed Expenses
Necessities
Desires

In the "Debts" column I kept track of what I owed and payments that I made to my creditors. Under "Fixed Expenses" I listed everything that had to be paid each month, including our monthly household rent. Under "Necessities" I listed the items we had to have to maintain our home and health—food, wood for heating and cooking, milk, medicine, candles for evening light, and similar things. The heading "Desires" listed all the items that were not necessary for the ongoing care of my family and home but objects we hoped to purchase when we were able, such as furniture, clothes, a carriage, and the like.

Once I had recorded all these figures in my booklet I then took action and began the actual disbursement of my funds.

Each month when I was paid I took four envelopes and marked one "Debts," another "Fixed Expenses," another "Necessities," and the last, "Desires." I first took ten percent of my income and put it into the "Debts" envelope, then sent the money to my creditors. From the balance, I put our rent money and other money for fixed expenses into the envelope marked "Fixed Expenses." Then I put sufficient funds to pay for our food and necessary items into the envelope marked "Necessities." As I mentioned, I carefully entered each of these sums in my memorandum book, keeping a running total each week and comparing the totals to my monthly available cash. The envelope marked "Desires" was the one I had to watch most carefully.

I quickly learned that this category held the key to the growth of my fortune. And I would soon learn that discipline is the mother of good luck. Or as Poor Richard once wrote, "There are no gains without pains."

Soon I was able to pay off all my creditors, which, I might add, reduced the worries which debt can cause. This gave us more available funds, as well as a good name, should I ever want to use their credit again, which I did later as I built my business.

When I paid off my debts I began a habit that would open the doors of prosperity and good luck for me. I began to tithe. I later increased my offerings and discovered that this habit indeed planted the seeds of prosperity for us.

I put my faith in the Scriptures, which said, "Give and it will be given to you. Good measure, pressed down, running over.

The measure that you give will be the measure that will be given to you."

Over the years I have found this wisdom to be true time and time again. As I gave more, I seemed to mysteriously earn more, which led me to give more, only to earn even more.

Then as the years went by and my wealth grew, I began to more fully understand that it is indeed more blessed to give than to receive.

Later in my years, I comprehended that a greater joy, happiness and fulfillment came from what I gave than from what I received. It was to take significant growth in wisdom tempered by my years before I began to fully understand this principle of prosperity.

Rebecca and I carefully disciplined ourselves to spend out of our "Desires" envelope only that which was available. Only after our fixed expenses, necessities and contributions were taken out would we allow ourselves to spend money on increased pleasures and only as we were able to pay for them in full.

We had to do without some things we wanted for a while after beginning this habit of budgeting our income and expenses. Though now I have no memory of feeling deprived. Instead, I remember feeling a great sense of relief, accomplishment and control of my own destiny. I felt good about my ability to live within my income. My fears subsided and my confidence abounded.

I was to discover in time that budgeting our income and expenses and refraining from spending money we did not possess truly laid the foundation for our accumulation of wealth. As I look back, I can clearly see that it was this step of learning through which we had to struggle before Providence blessed us with increased fortunes. A passage I might add, that many people never steer themselves through.

We learned from the adage: "Our spending mysteriously increases so as to devour all our available income!" Prosperity and abundance began to favor us when we resolved to trim our expenses to weigh less than our income.

This monetary discipline, although not comfortable at first, paved the way for the wealth that lay ahead.

The Third Law of Wealth and Abundance

Trim Your Expenses to Weigh Less Than Your Income

Write each expenditure you make. Develop a plan to pay off all debts. Be sure to allow yourself enough time to do it with a fixed percentage of your income. Pay that first. Divide your remaining funds into "Fixed Expenses," "Necessities," and "Desires." Pay your "Fixed Expenses" first, then your "Necessities." Purchase no "Desire" items such as luxuries unless you have the money left over with which to pay for them in full. When your debts are paid off, give a minimum of ten percent to the place of worship or charities of your choice. This habit will further cause you to plant the seeds to yield future financial freedom. It will pave the way for the next law of prosperity and abundance which I will reveal in the following chapter. The momentary discomfort of this discipline will help you enjoy a life full of abundance.

Chapter 4

THE FOURTH LAW OF WEALTH AND ABUNDANCE

SET ASIDE FOR YOURSELF A PART OF EVERYTHING YOU EARN

Small amounts regularly saved
is how the road to wealth is paved.

Those were indeed exciting times for Rebecca and myself. Our lives were truly filled with wonderful events. Mr. Whitworth's newly expanded mercantile store was growing with the city. Our family had just celebrated Benjamin's first birthday. He was beginning to talk and to walk. We were happy, so content, so full of hopes and dreams for the future.

I designed a sensible budget system, and for several months we strictly adhered to it. We became debt-free, establishing ourselves as worthy, prudent citizens. Our confidence and optimism for the future were rising with our financial security.

There was but one area that continually nagged me—our lack of savings. It seemed that by the end of each month we had only a few coins that were available to put into our savings.

I felt frustrated because of my desires to some day own my own business. I knew that without sufficient savings I would never be able to reach this dream. "I shall never amass any significant amount of money," I complained to Rebecca on several occasions.

I remember telling myself every month that this was the time we would begin a savings fund. However, it seemed that each time we decided that we must have and deserved some home improvement. Such as new curtains, along with new whitewash, a new rug, and some paintings for our walls.

My own youthful pride, along with my love for Rebecca and Benjamin, caused me to want the best for them. This desire to rise above my beginnings, I would later discover, also caused me to wish to appear as prosperous to Rebecca's family members.

Although our fancied-up surroundings made us feel comfortable and extremely proud, we were still bothered by the fact that this course of spending did nothing to increase our savings.

For many long hours Rebecca and I discussed our values, desires, and choices. We finally acknowledged in ourselves a natural inclination to want to purchase things that other people we knew were acquiring and enjoying.

It came to us that just before we made the choices to improve our little house, Rebecca's older brother, Clinton, had come into a financial upturn.

For ten years he had owned a shop that made wagon wheels. As had the mercantile store, it prospered as our fair city of Philadelphia and all of the colonies grew. One day a group of investors offered him a sizable profit for the sale of his business. Seizing upon this fortunate opportunity, he quickly agreed to sell it to them for an amount that was beyond many of our dreams.

After the sale, he and his family enjoyed his newfound riches for several months. They purchased a much larger home, a new carriage, and new furnishings. They boarded a steamer ship for London, where they spent two months in a fine hotel. They reveled in their newfound—and ultimately, I'm sad to say, temporary—wealth.

A strange sensation arose in Rebecca and me as we watched intently and enviously as Clinton and his family satisfied some of their—and our—pent-up desires. We acknowledged that we, too, wanted to have what they had and to go places where they were going. In fact, these events created a strong urge within us to take what little accumulated savings we had and lavish it on ourselves as they had done, hence the curtains, whitewash, and pictures. But then good sense prevailed and we stiffened our resolve to increase our luxuries only from our "Desires" envelope, and that the amount placed in that envelope was to be determined only after paying ten percent to savings and giving another ten percent to charity.

We pledged to end our spending spree and to return to our savings habit, not robbing it to purchase goods that offered only fleeting values. We agreed that we would not make spending decisions that were motivated by envy. Instead we would trust our belief that our current sacrifices would one day lead to greater riches.

We learned an enduring lesson as we watched Clinton foolishly squander his wealth. As it turned out, he was to receive the money for his business in four payments—one-fourth down and an equal one fourth each year hence for three years. Knowing that he had the reserve of three more payments, he saw little need to be careful with the money from the first installment. Sadly, this was mostly gone by the time he came back from London.

Upon returning, he quickly discovered that the purchaser of his business had not been a person of integrity and had quickly liquidated his business and fled the colonies with the money. Poor Clinton was left with neither money nor a business with which to make money. Suffice it to say he suffered deep regrets for his foolish and extravagant spending habits.

Observing this, I was indeed shocked into the realization that an unfortunate circumstance could also happen to me. I resolved to begin a reserve for such an occurrence. It was a sobering lesson for me to learn. To watch the pain, embarrassment, and humiliation on the faces of Clinton and his good wife served as a clarion warning to me that I would never erase from my mind.

This experience proved the advice of Poor Richard who wrote: "Buy what thou hast no need of, and ere long thou shalt sell thy necessities."

As Rebecca and I hurt for poor Clinton, I was suddenly struck with an understanding of the wisdom that Mr. Franklin had not too long before given me.

This memory was painfully accompanied by my admission that I had only heard his wisdom, but, unfortunately, had not applied it. I clearly remember now how I had reviewed for him my budgeting activities. He complimented me for my initiative. It was then that he interspersed his conversation with these words of Poor Richard as he loved to do: "Small amounts regularly saved is how the road to wealth is paved."

I always relished the moments when Mr. Franklin shifted into his alter ego, Richard Saunders. It was as if he donned a whole new countenance. His facial expressions, smile, and gestures changed noticeably. He preceded each quote from Poor Richard by smiling, then looking upward and repeating his favorite sayings. He made his point and then looked squarely into my eyes, I suppose to see if I had comprehended his words. Then he would finish with a self-effacing chuckle, throw his hand outward and remark, "Old men love to give advice, you know!"

Although this was over thirty years ago, I remember still his countenance and every one of his unique mannerisms.

Oh, what wonderful memories I hold from my visits with this great man, and how clearly I can now trace the vast wealth I have accumulated from those early learning experiences. Surely, few people in history have enjoyed such a wise teacher. Ah, yes, those were such wonderful years.

I remember how Mr. Franklin had made me aware of this law of savings during one of our early encounters. When I first began a budgeting process I reviewed with him the amounts I had specified for "Fixed Expenses," "Necessities," "Charity" and "Desires." He then mentioned one of his repeated sayings: "To be wealthy you must think of saving as well as getting."

I recall that I listened to his words, but I must have looked disappointed. I had been so proud that I had found a way to pay for all our expenses out of my wages. Now he was telling me that I needed to search even further within the seemingly paltry amount.

As if sensing my feelings, he inquired, "Do I bring up a point which frustrates you?"

"Well...sir...to be honest, I have thought of saving. I think of it often, in fact, but simply thinking about it does little good. When I examine my budget I do not know from where any more money would come. I do not see how I can do much else but think of it at this time. I know I need to begin a savings habit, but, well, I have just never been able to establish one."

How could I ever forget that day he confronted me and forced me to admit my procrastination. "So you view saving as something you will do in the future when you earn more money?" he challenged. He then paused as he watched me nodding forlornly. "Tell me," he went on, "of your present earnings as a clerk, do you put any of it into savings?"

"Well, sir," I said, looking down and fumbling with a pad and pencil, "not much...not much, I'm afraid."

"Tell me how much," he pressed.

"Well...frankly sir...I have no savings," I admitted, and I felt the flush of embarrassment rise over my face.

"And how long have you been a clerk?"

"I...I am on my sixth year now, sir."

"And in six years you have saved nothing?" he asked directly.

"Yes," I admitted. "I am afraid that is true. As you know I got married, and we had a baby. We needed a larger house and more furniture. . ."

"None of those excuses will do, young man. The real problem is that you have not been thinking of saving as well as getting!"

"But sir, I think of it constantly! My heart is often filled with fears of unexpected tragedy or illness that might strike me or my family. This fear has caused me to resolve, many times, to begin a reserve for such events. But it always seems that all I can do is stretch my income to barely meet our expenses."

Although I was afraid of further scolding, apparently Mr. Franklin heard the sincere frustration in my voice and, after a moment of silence, smiled warmly. "You share a common problem with many others, my young friend. People of both substantial and modest incomes are troubled by the same malady—that of spending all they earn.

"As I have said before," he went on, "Our spending mysteriously increases so as to devour all of our available income."

Saying this he eyed me for a moment. "And yet I have observed that those of us who put our minds to it usually achieve what we want most to have! If our desire to spend exceeds our desire to save, we will accumulate little of real value. But if our desire to save exceeds our desire to spend, we will accumulate much, regardless of the size of our beginning. 'Great oaks, you know, from small acorns grow,'" he said, shifting into the role of Poor Richard for a moment.

"However, for an acorn to grow, it must first be planted. It must have a start, a beginning. And if you truly desire wealth, you must make a start, and you are the only one who can make a decision to begin."

He paused for a moment, watching as I took in his words. "As I have told you before, 'Small amounts regularly saved is how the road to wealth is paved!' However, you must also remember that there are many roadblocks to saving. You must recognize these difficulties and find a way to get beyond them. That is indeed the price you must pay before increased prosperity can ever visit you. You must also learn to make your expenses a servant to your discipline, to trim these so they weigh less than your income. Discipline, you know, is indeed the mother of good luck."

"But, sir," I still remember interrupting him, "All this is easy for you to say, for you are already wealthy. It is simple to advise others to save money when you have much yourself!"

My brashness soon caused me to feel foolish for what I had said to him. I realized my outburst was given rise by my inclination to blame circumstances and not take full responsibility for my actions.

His words, "Discipline is the mother of good luck", as all his wisdom has a way of doing, cut through my excuses and caused me to face the realities of my own choices.

Although it has been years since this happened, I still remember how he looked at me. I suspected by the look in his eyes that he was assessing whether or not I had the will to get beyond my excuses and embrace what he said. It suddenly struck me that he might be at a decision point, that maybe he was deciding whether to invest any more of his time and experience in me, that he was wondering if I was willing to learn to listen and take action on his advice.

"My young friend," he finally said in a stern manner, "do you choose to wallow in the comfort of excusing your lack of discipline...or do you have the courage to choose to change your lot in life?"

He had never talked to me with this tone of voice before. I felt impaled by his question. I cast down my eyes for a long moment, and during that silence I reached into the very bottom of my soul to see for myself what substance I possessed.

At once I knew that if this great man believed in my potential for success, that if he invested his time in me, that I should not disappoint him. I raised my chin and said, "Sir, please forgive me. I apologize for my lack of wisdom and my resistance. I have apparently been listening only with my ears, but today I assure you that I am listening with my heart as well. Please continue."

Mr. Franklin relaxed once again into the chair where he sat. "If you truly desire wealth, you must learn to weigh every small expense and nothing waste, for pennies long saved amount to pounds with haste! Then by industry and ambition, you will increase your available dollars. If you but develop this habit of saving, you will be well on the road to wealth. My friend, the man who has a surplus in savings is master of many situations. He is the slave to no one. And you will cease to be a slave to circumstances when you truly learn that to be wealthy you must think of saving as well as getting!"

His confrontation had hit its mark—the very center of my being. I was cut to my core by his question that day. It exposed my excuses and my lack of discipline; it brought me face to face with the decision point: Would I truly take control of my financial future or would I continue to live in a state of denial?

Fortunately, I made the better choice, a decision that would indeed lay the foundation for my future wealth. It was here I was to learn a most fundamental truth: It was not the amount of money I saved that was primary in importance, but the habits I formed that contributed so largely to my future wealth.

I was soon to make two important discoveries. One was that when saving becomes a priority, you begin to discover previously unrecognizable ways to do it. My needs to spend and acquire began to subside, yielding in importance to my strong desire to build a surplus for my future business plans.

My other discovery was that later when I needed borrowed capital for my business, my bankers were so impressed with my ability and discipline that they did not hesitate to lend me the funds I needed. I later came to understand that a man's character is one of the prime concerns of money lenders.

Although the years now separate us, I vividly remember this momentous visit with Mr. Franklin. He had that day caused no small degree of challenge and excitement in me; his words encouraged me to rekindle my efforts and energies. Although I had previously understood his words, the importance of his message had failed to sink into my slow mind until that great day.

I began immediately to repeat the phrase he taught me in that meeting: "To be wealthy I must think of saving as well as getting." I repeated this sentence again and again to keep it foremost in my mind.

Each time I spent a few coins for milk or food, I thought of his words. When I paid the rent, I thought of them again. I thought of his words when I paid the cobbler, the baker and the candle maker.

In no time at all I developed the habit of questioning each expenditure I made. Soon I preceded all of my expenditures with the question, "How may I save instead of spend?" In doing so I discovered that many pennies slipped through my fingers needlessly. I soon found that I could survive on less than I had previously thought necessary, without suffering any discomfort.

Rebecca and I became indeed willing to favor frugality in order to speed up our future prosperity. We looked for ways to conserve.

We discovered that we could, by wise selection, save on our food. Rebecca's family had a plot of ground they allowed us to cultivate as a garden in the summer. Not only were we able to enjoy healthy foods in season, but we also put away foods for winter.

We then played games with each other. When we saw something that we wanted to purchase which we would have previously purchased, we said to each other, "Let's pay ourselves rather than this merchant!" We then took that amount and put it into our savings account.

After several months went by, I came to understand I had been a slave to the circumstances of my life instead of their master. I had simply not chosen to control my destiny. I also realized I expected to end each month with nothing left over, and since I expected to have nothing, that was what I realized. I immediately determined to elevate myself from that demeaning station in life. To do this, I resolved to take a modest percentage of my weekly pay and deposit it with a respectable banker. This I did, although at first it seemed such a paltry amount. Soon I recognized we did not miss the money, as somehow I was still able to provide for my family after setting aside my savings.

When I discovered the ease of this habit, I decided to make it a permanent part of my budget and routine. I resolved I would be true to myself and not cheat myself by watching all my earnings flow into the pockets of other people. I pledged that before I spent anything on my own desires I would set money aside for myself.

As time went on, I discovered I was able to increase the amount I put into savings more easily than I previously thought possible. Before long, I found I had developed a new confidence. I had a different feeling about myself. I held myself in higher esteem. I felt more like a man of substance and worth.

Soon a new joy flowed all through me, a joy that gave me even more determination; it gave me more confidence in my abilities and in my future. This one habit, more than any others, laid the foundation for the wealth I was later to build. Indeed, without this firm habit of saving, no solid success would have ever been built.

As the years passed and I visited with many people to discuss wealth and prosperity, I came to realize that although most people know they should save money, they do not actually do it. They never take it from knowing to doing, from thoughts to habits; and so they suffer from all sorts of problems that would have otherwise been prevented.

Even when they make a commitment to save, many find reasons to wait until next month or next year or some other future date to begin. Many people postpone their success by saying, "I know that it is important to save but I cannot begin now. I have bills to pay and there are things I need to buy!" I played at this game, too, but I now understand that there is never a convenient time to begin; one must just choose to save and then do it!

There is also another problem I have seen and experienced. Even when a person resolves to begin a savings plan, they attempt at first to save unrealistically large amounts of money. Because the amount is not reasonable for their budget and spending needs, they soon run into difficulties. This leads to discouragement, and before they realize what has happened, they have abandoned the whole project, never to try again.

As Poor Richard said: "'Tis easy to make a bold resolution, but the difficulty is in the execution!"

I have experienced many of the roadblocks that hinder people in their savings plans. I know all of the excuses. My fortunes took a decidedly different turn only on the day I made a firm resolve to close the door on my denial and lack of discipline, and open it to my future prosperity. On that day I decided to take my life in my own hands, to set aside for myself a part of everything I earned.

Let me repeat the substance of my lesson: It was not the amount of money I saved which was most important, it was the habit of regularly saving that paved the road for my future wealth. It was proving to myself and others that I could indeed be the master of my money. I learned from Mr. Franklin that "Small amounts regularly saved is how the road to wealth is paved."

Yes, as the great man told me many years ago, "If you would be wealthy, you must think of saving as well as getting."

To gain much, you must remember this law of wealth and abundance: *Set aside for yourself a part of everything you earn!*

This habit will indeed lay a solid foundation for your future prosperity.

THE FOURTH LAW OF WEALTH AND ABUNDANCE

SET ASIDE FOR YOURSELF A PART OF EVERYTHING YOU EARN

Before you pay anyone else, first pay yourself. Do not allow your hard-earned funds to flow into the pockets of other people. Understand that there will never be a convenient time to start saving. Understand, also, that the major obstacle of saving is simply that of getting started. Set realistic aspirations for yourself, even if the amount is small. Allow nothing to block your future success by causing you to spend your savings dollars. Learn to spend your money on tangible things that last. Avoid expenditures that are eaten up, worn out, or that are consumed quickly. Do not be deceived by the apparent slowness of your savings build up. In time you will see small beginnings grow into significant amounts. Remember, "Small amounts regularly saved is how the road to wealth is paved."

B. FRANKLIN
PRINTER
STATIONER
PENNSYLVANIA
GAZETTE
LEGAL BLANKS

Chapter 5

THE FIFTH LAW OF WEALTH AND ABUNDANCE

INCREASE YOUR INCOME BY MULTIPLYING YOUR VALUE TO OTHERS

One day Mr. Franklin sent a messenger to the shop to invite me to join him and two other young men for an evening of talk in his home. I was, of course, delighted and thrilled to have become so familiar with this great gentleman that he would invite me into his home.

I ran home after work to tell Rebecca, who I knew would be as excited as I at my opportunity. She was, and then pointed out in her always perceptive way, "See, Andrew, Mr. Franklin would not be spending all this time helping you to improve yourself and our position in life if he did not believe in you." I could see what seemed like pride shining in her eyes as she kissed me good-bye.

We gathered in Franklin Court, the marvelous house which Franklin had built. While away in England during much of the construction of the great house, he nevertheless had sent his wife Deborah many detailed letters about the finishing of it.

As far as I knew he was the first person in the city to have an indoor flush facility that one used instead of an outhouse. He was rather proud of that device and predicted that in future times every home would have one. Few people believed him and thought him too eccentric, though I have no doubt what he said will become true one day.

That evening I purposefully arrived at Mr. Franklin's home a few minutes earlier than the others, taking any opportunity I could to spend a few moments alone with this great man, for these moments were always filled with fascination and adventure. On this particular evening, he led me into the parlor, then pointed to a strange piece of furniture in the corner. "Look at my new musical instrument," Mr. Franklin said with pride. "A friend who is a member of the Royal Society in London sent it to me."

The contraption looked like a sideboard on long legs with a big wheel on the left-hand side. A treadle board extended from the wheel to the floor so that the wheel could be turned by foot. Stooping down to look under the wheel I saw many glasses filled to different levels with water. "What is it?" I asked, enthralled.

"It is an armonica, a very, very popular instrument in London. Let me show you how it works."

Saying this he spun the wheel with his left hand and then began to pump the treadle board, which turned a large cylindrical shaft with grooves on it. The grooves made contact with the glasses to make strange and somewhat eerie sounds.

He chortled with delight as he watched my reaction to the armonica's unique music, then he said, "A skilled performer published a set of instructions for playing it, though I have not yet mastered the thing. However, I already see that there are ways to simplify it so it can be played with more ease and clarity. I am going to work on that problem and make improvements on it."

Mr. Franklin spent many hours redesigning this intriguing instrument. One evening, several months later, he showed me a letter he had written to the famous Italian scientist and writer, Giovanni Battista Beccaria, explaining how he had improved the instrument.

During the next few years, the armonica became quite popular on the Continent. Two of Franklin's friends, Marianne and Cecilia Davies, gave public concerts all across Europe, culminating in Vienna, where they played the armonica at the marriage of Archduchess Amalia and Duke Ferdinand of Parma. The popular Wolfgang Amadeus Mozart and Ludwig van Beethoven both composed music for the instrument.

Franklin's inventive genius was legend. Among his many successes in this field, he did, in 1747, construct a crude electrical generator. Later, in 1751 to be exact, he published his first edition of his *Experiments and Observations in Electricity*. His progress in the study of electricity was neither simple nor easy, as he spent several years working in this new science. He strived to prove that lightning and electricity were the same. His vision was that as lightning illuminates the sky, so could electricity, provided it could be harnessed.

However, one of his great frustrations was that he could never find a practical way to transform electricity into sustained light.

Praised by many for his discoveries and beliefs, he was also soundly denounced by others as "doing devilish work." Certain religious sects stoutly accused him of going against the will of God.

Once again, I observed with astonishment that a man who had the genius to discover so many new inventions and who moved with the most famous people in the world would take his time to help me learn.

Allow me to go back to one evening when I was a guest in Mr. Franklin's house. As Samuel Kingsley and Arnold Vaughn arrived, we retreated to the drawing room. These two young men were about my age and in the same station in life. I discovered that for several years Mr. Franklin had silently practiced the habit of finding young men in whom he detected strong desires for achievement and spending time with them. He would take time out of his busy life to assist the learning of others. This gave testimony to his desire to perpetuate his wisdom.

I suspected, though, that it was even more than that, and in fact, was simply a manifestation of his character. He genuinely wanted to make the world a better place in which to live and to repay for the blessings he richly enjoyed.

Where had he met the two young men who joined us that evening? He never told me. All I knew is that we each had strong ambitions and a desire to learn the ways to wealth. Mr. Franklin recognized this and had agreed to instruct us on this arduous journey, as long, of course, as we showed a willingness to practice what we learned.

Benefits a-plenty would come from these meetings and from Franklin's tutelage. Samuel Kingsley became president of the University of Pennsylvania, and Arnold Vaughn served as a noted circuit judge, while I, as I have mentioned before, found success in the business world, amassing a fortune in shipping and commerce. However, on this evening in Mr. Franklin's home, we were but eager students of this great man who so influenced our way in life.

"It is time," Mr. Franklin said, after we were settled into our seats, "for you to take the next step in building your wealth. Now that you are controlling your appetites and setting aside savings for your future prosperity, you shall each advance to the point of increasing your income. Building on the foundation you have laid, you will now be able to stack brick after brick into a wall of wealth and financial security.

"However," he emphasized, "be forewarned! If you let that foundation of saving and budgeting crumble, you will see your walls come tumbling down as well. If you increase your income without continuing to control your expenses you will only see all your newly earned dollars, regardless of the amount, flowing into other people's pockets. Remember," he concluded as he pointed his finger into the air, "our spending mysteriously increases so as to devour all our available income!"

I had heard that before and, as I suspected, the others had also. We nodded our heads to show our understanding.

"Well, now, I asked you all here because I thought we should spend the evening discussing how each of you can increase your income, how you can begin immediately to earn more money. Andrew, let's begin with you. How will you increase your income?"

I paused for a moment, trying to think of something to say. Then I decided that, as usual, I must be honest with this great man, for he could always see through my bluffs. "I am afraid, sir, that I am experiencing difficulty seeing how I can increase my income substantially. My employer already pays me a salary that is more than twice what he was paying when you and I first met, and I am working ever so much harder than I was at that time. There are no more hours left in the day for me to work at anything else."

"So is there no solution to your problem?" he pressed. "Are you willing to settle for life as it is now?"

As he asked this question, his eyes drilled into me and let me know that he would not accept my excuses.

"Forgive my being blunt with you, Andrew, but we have been in discussion long enough now that I owe you honesty and directness. Most people advance no further in life than where they are because they find it difficult to see themselves going where they have never been! But, my friend," and he pointed his finger directly at me, "as that all-wise, all-knowing Poor Richard was so fond of writing, 'Where there's a will, there's a way!'"

He sat back and chuckled, which relaxed the somewhat tense atmosphere of the room. It had been almost ten years since Mr. Franklin had written his last *Poor Richard's Almanacks*. They had made him the most popular man in the colonies, and he still loved to speak through the character of his own invention.

Looking at the three of us, Mr. Franklin went on. "Most often, the route to increased income lies not in looking for new fields but in looking in your own backyard. Let me emphasize that increased earnings almost always follow increased productivity. Wealth grows when we become more productive!"

"But, Mr. Franklin," Samuel Kingsley responded, "like Andrew just said, there are only so many hours in a day. How can we be more productive when we are already working six long days each week?"

"Oh, young friend," Mr. Franklin smiled, "there's a difference between just working and being your most productive. Many people are content to put in their time. Their objective is to work a specified number of hours and then go to their homes.

"However," he continued, "people who enjoy increased prosperity concern themselves with filling their hours with fruitful results instead of just filling the hours. My friends, opportunity is everywhere. It reveals itself, however, only to those who look for it. Most of my own success came from recognizing opportunity—opportunity from circumstances, as well as from people.

"Let me give you an example. In 1724, at the age of eighteen, I sailed to England with my friend, James Ralph. On the day that we passed Chelsea, where the famous architect Christopher Wren had rebuilt the old theological college into a hospital, we took time to visit this inspiring edifice.

"Intrigued with Wren's genius, I wanted to see as much of his work as I could. Well, on our return to the ship, I impulsively stripped, leapt into the river, and swam from near Chelsea to Blackfriars. I had for years been delighted with the exercise of swimming, which I had practiced as a boy, when I had studied the book called *The Art of Swimming*, written around 1699 by Mechisedech Theirnot.

"It seems that, not gifted with that marvelous trait of humility, I took this occasion to exhibit my skills to the bystanders on the shore, and I was much flattered by their admiration.

"Well, one spectator, a gentleman named Denham, desirous to improve his own aquatic skills, became quite attached to me. Mr. Denham had previously been in business in Bristol, England, had failed and settled his debts with his creditors by compromising and paying them less than they were due. He then sailed to America and by close application of his business, he acquired a fortune in just a few years.

"He returned to England on the same ship with me. After we arrived in London, he included me in a most elegant dinner, to which he invited his creditors. There he thanked them for their settlement a few years earlier, then served them a most enjoyable feast. They appreciated their host's gratitude and expected nothing else, but then Mr. Denham asked each of them to look under his plate. There they found a bank order for the full amount that they had been due, plus interest.

"Now, excuse my rambling, my young friends," he apologized, looking over his spectacles. "You will understand my point in time. Sometime after this spectacular dinner, my friend Denham proposed that I go to work with him, that we go back to Philadelphia and that I become his clerk, keep his books, copy his letters, and attend his store. He added that if I became acquainted with the mercantile business he would promote me by sending me with a cargo of flour and grain to the West Indies and that he would pay commissions, which would be very profitable for me. I eagerly agreed to join him in this business venture.

"So on the twenty-third of July, 1726, we sailed from England to Pennsylvania. We landed in Philadelphia on the eleventh of October. We took a store on Water Street, where we displayed our goods. I attended to business with diligence, studied accounts, and in a short time, grew expert at selling.

"All during this time Mr. Denham counseled me as a father, having a sincere regard for me. He quickly saw that I was quite willing to work extra hours and apply myself to learning the ways of creating profits.

"We were doing quite well together. I loved him and I loved the work and we might have gone on for many years except for a most unfortunate tragedy. In February 1727, we both developed pleurisy, which very nearly carried me off, and sadly enough, killed my good friend.

"At his death he left me a legacy as a token of his kindness and regard. I was surprised, but learned a great lesson that, I might add, has served me well many times since.

"Well," he chuckled, "Old men love to hear themselves talk, you know. But tell me, young friends, what lessons did you discover in my story?"

Then, just as easily as Mr. Franklin rolled out the stories, he became quiet and waited for us to talk. We all three looked at each other, daring the others to be the first to speak. Samuel finally spoke up. "Well, sir, I suppose...I suppose one point I discovered in your story is that...well, when you are good at something, people will often admire you and want to help you improve your lot in life."

"That is, indeed, a truth, Samuel."

"And," Arnold spoke up, "that opportunity shows itself in unusual places."

"That is very perceptive, Arnold. Andrew, how about you, what lessons have you learned from my story?"

I thought for a moment before speaking. "I suppose I was not thinking so much of lessons as...well, I did not know that you once worked in a mercantile store on Water Street."

"Yes, yes, I did."

"How long ago, sir?"

"How long? Well, many years now. Let me think...that was in 1726...so it has been over fifty years now. But, back to my question, Andrew, what points did you see in my story?"

"Well, sir, it seems to me that when you did a good job for Mr. Denham, he trusted you and...had confidence in you and then offered you more opportunities to earn..."

"And more responsibilities, too," Samuel added.

"Yes, yes, you all make good points. What else?"

Samuel said, "When you assume the responsibility of overseeing other people, you stand the chance of making more money."

"That's very interesting, Samuel," Mr. Franklin said, and it was clear from his tone that he had not really meant to leave that message.

Everyone sat quietly for a moment. Smiling at Samuel, Mr. Franklin went on, "My main point, my young friends, is that when you place yourselves in situations where influential people are, and when you demonstrate skills that they find desirable, you increase your chances of success. But, there is another idea that I want to share with you. It is this: 'Prosperity often increases when we use our time wisely.'

"Poor Richard wrote, 'We are taxed twice as much for our idleness.' I have also observed that we are rewarded twice for our initiative, thrice for our industry, and four times for our diligence.

"Allow me," he went on, "to ask each of you to spend the next fortnight making application of the following statement: 'Make every hour do the work of two!'

"I have noticed," he went on, "that many people squander time without the awareness that they are squandering life and opportunity. Time is money. Squander time and you squander the stuff life is made of.

"As a young tradesman, after establishing myself, my next task was to increase my results by multiplying my effectiveness in using my time. I soon learned the value of industry and initiative. I vowed to have my creditors see lights in the window and hear noise in my printing shop as they went to work early in the morning as well as when they went home in the evening.

"Until I could afford to hire other craftsman, I first determined to make every hour do the work of two. I learned that he who rises late must trot all day and shall scarce overtake his business at night."

Saying this he paused to pick up a small stack of blank cards. "In fact," he went on, handing each of us one of the cards and pushing an ink stand and quill closer to us, "might I ask each of you to write this statement on your cards? 'Make every hour do the work of two,'" he repeated slowly.

He shifted in his chair, leaned on his cane and held his left knee with his hand seemingly to ease the pressure on his foot for a moment. Then he turned his attention to his instruction again.

"Might I also suggest that each of you carry this little card with you for the next fortnight. Read the card several times each day. Ask yourself many times each day, 'How can I make every hour do the work of two?'

"At first, you may find few answers to your questions. But keep asking. And if you ask long enough, you will surely begin to get answers.

"Which brings up the third point I wanted to make with my story: Concern yourself with getting results, rather than just doing your job.

"Increase the results for almost anyone and they will be happy to allow you to share in the increase. To increase your productivity so that you increase your income, consider creating more results and profits for your employer.

"Then, to become more wealthy, discover ways to multiply this. Learn how to manage other people so they become more productive. The more people you lead to greater productivity, the more you will be paid.

"Ultimately, my young friends, you will be rewarded for the total productivity you cause to happen. Produce well yourself, and you will be rewarded accordingly. Work through other people and you will be paid according to your overall increase in productivity. Wealth increases as you lead the greatest number of people into levels of productivity.

"Well," he said, shifting again in his chair, "you surely have heard enough of this old man's harangue. But before you go, tell me, as a result of what you have learned this evening, what will you do now? What lessons will find their way into your practice?"

Each of us thought over his question and responded, making a commitment to him of how we would make one hour do the work of two.

In a few minutes, he dismissed us. I assumed he was tired and needed his rest, though as we left, I heard the strange sounds of the armonica. Standing in the street outside his home, Samuel and I looked at each other, then Samuel winked, smiled and pointed to Mr. Franklin's home.

My mind was filled with many ideas after that night. As always, after time spent with Mr. Franklin, I promised myself I would not allow this famous man's investment of time to go to waste.

As I shared with Rebecca that night, I took from his story three points, three ways that I could increase my work habits and thereby increase my income. I committed to each of these.

They were:

1. To continue to learn as much as I could about account-keeping and successful management.
2. To accept responsibility for increasing the sales of all our clerks by managing and training them in a more effective manner.
3. To increase the profits of our store through better purchasing practices.

At first I did not know exactly how I would accomplish each of these three commitments. But I remembered what Mr. Franklin had said, and I kept thinking of them and turned them over to that inner part of my mind that sends me ideas and insights and trusted that part of me to search for ways to achieve them.

It was as if that Inner Wisdom deeply buried within me was just waiting for me to ask it for direction, for in almost no time I began to get answers in the form of hunches and ideas. I asked Mr. Whitworth to allow me to assume overall management of our store. Not only the clerks, but responsibilities for both sales and profits. He asked why I wanted to do this and I explained my desire to increase my success and to hone my business skills. I knew that if I increased the shop's profits he would be delighted to increase my income.

He gladly agreed, saying that he would continue to pay me a part of the increased sales as bonus, as well as also paying me a portion of our increased profits.

This would increase my earnings possibilities, if, of course, I could create increases in profits. It was here that I was to learn a great lesson that as soon as I prepared myself and accepted more responsibilities for results that the opportunity opened itself up to me.

I was to observe this phenomenon many times. As I grew to a new level of learning and productivity, new opportunities I had not previously recognized were suddenly revealed to me. I learned that when the student is ready, the teacher appears.

My enthusiasm and optimistic spirit helped me to perform my work more efficiently. My willingness to do extra work and to spend extra hours soon endeared me even more to Mr. Whitworth. At the same time, as Mr. Franklin advised, I continued with my habit of saving one-tenth of my income.

In a short time, Mr. Whitworth was stricken with a sudden seizure and was immobilized for a period of time before prematurely passing from this life. His widow then relied solely on me as the manager of the business. This continued for a while until, desiring funds to take care of herself in her old age, she allowed me to purchase the business. I was able to use the savings I had accumulated as surplus capital for the business and agreed to pay her a fixed amount from our future profits.

"I would not trust just anyone, Andrew," I remember her telling me. "But I know you are a person of integrity and industry. In the years you have worked in our store, we learned we can trust you and that you have the many skills which successful management requires."

Since then I have learned many lessons about being more productive: How to multiply myself by having others do jobs for me; how to increase productivity by training people to be more skillful; how to provide products and services that contribute to the health and enjoyment of others; and that prosperity is increased by bringing buyers and sellers together. I have learned that solving larger problems leads to proportional increases in the income I earn, and that almost anyone can find ways to be more productive.

I learned I must first choose the level of income and prosperity I want to enjoy, then decide the level of productivity I must make happen myself or through other people. I learned that to enjoy more wealth, I only need to increase my level of productivity to open the door to receive it.

Yes, as we become more productive we cause the doors of wealth and prosperity to open to us.

Wealth grows when we become more productive.

THE FIFTH LAW OF WEALTH AND ABUNDANCE

INCREASE YOUR INCOME BY MULTIPLYING YOUR VALUE TO OTHERS

Ask yourself each day, "How can I make one hour do the work of two?" Keep records of how and on what you spend your time. Ask yourself each day, "What results can I make happen?" not "How can I get through this day?" Learn to delegate and get more done by having others do jobs for you. Look at your present position and ask yourself, "How can I do my job more efficiently?" Place yourself in an environment where there are successful people. Strive to create more value for your employer, clients, customers or patients. Make your motto, "Before I can expect to get more, I first need to give more!" In every generation, those individuals who prosper the most are the ones who most efficiently fill the needs of the greatest number of people.

Chapter 6

THE SIXTH LAW OF WEALTH AND ABUNDANCE

INVEST WITH THE GREATEST PRUDENCE AND SAFETY

Keeping your wealth requires thrice the diligence than the effort to earn it.

Time moved rapidly for me, filled with so many memories. Exciting events happened to us, both personally and business wise. One only has to look back over the years to appreciate how the richness of both struggle and success are often overlooked in the busy press of life.

One pleasant memory tarnished by sadness which stands out in my mind was when Benjamin was seven. For his birthday I purchased a pony for him to ride. A gray and beautiful pony. It was obvious from the first sighting that the two were to become quite closely attached.

Rebecca bought riding clothing for our son. Polished black knee-high riding boots, loden Irish linen jodhpurs and jacket, a mustard-colored waistcoat, shirt cuffs that puffed out from his coat sleeves. He felt and looked so elegant!

It was a time made more special when we reflected on the sadness of the two miscarriages that Rebecca had suffered, never to bear another child.

Benjamin named the horse "Whinney," for the sound she made when she first saw him each morning. They were inseparable. It was such a joy to witness the times they had together.

One day Benjamin was riding Whinney when a rabbit jumped out of the grass and spooked the horse, who shied and reared, throwing Benjamin from the saddle, breaking his arm. When we found him lying on the ground he attempted to be so brave by hiding his tears. His mother and I had no such success hiding ours.

His broken arm would indeed heal, but unfortunately would never be straight again.

I was later to learn it is the bitter sweetness of life's experiences that gives our blessings meaning and makes them special. For it was the tragedy of a deformed arm that would later lead our son into his chosen profession. One, I might add, that would eventually help improve the health of thousands of people.

By now some time had gone by since I purchased the business from Mr. Whitworth's widow. We were blessed with continued prosperity and growth.

Although the days moved so quickly, seemingly not allowing me to have extra time, I nevertheless carefully carved out specific moments each day to reflect on my rich blessings. I had often taken special notice that people who seemed to experience extra measures of joy and happiness were also people who routinely demonstrated a thankful spirit. I have since come to accept as fact that a thankful spirit turns all it touches into happiness. Another observation I have made is that each of us has a choice as to what type of thoughts we select to think and that our thoughts are powerful enough to transform themselves into their physical equivalent. I learned that a thankful spirit is like a magnet—attracting people and prosperity to us.

My moments of thanksgiving often caused me to reflect on my childhood. In that two-room house, growing up with five brothers and three sisters, never having all the food we wanted or needed. I still remember the cold, the hand-me-down clothes, the well-worn shoes that never seemed adequate to keep out the snow during the wet Philadelphia winters.

Little did I know, when I first began to work in Mr. Whitworth's merchandise store as a young clerk, that I would someday own several stores, buildings and property. That I would own sailing ships that traded tobacco, cotton, gold, silver, indigo and furs for such things as fine English linens and china, along with Scottish woolens and beautiful crystal from Sweden. We imported many other luxuries as well, such as exquisite silks from the Orient, gleaming gemstones from Brazil, tea from Ceylon and all kinds of spices from India.

Indeed, my trade empire was to eventually fill many warehouses and employ several hundred people.

As my business became established, Rebecca and I moved into a beautiful two-story home on Walnut Street. We were to spend many happy moments there until, some years later, we built the mansion that sits high above the Schuylkill.

The home on Walnut Street was a reward for our previous years of frugality and savings. It seemed so elegant. Rebecca personally chose all the furniture and fabrics. The kitchen with its huge hearth and the garden filled with beautiful bursts of color in the spring and summer became the setting of many happy memories. Several people who were to become well-known lived nearby, such as Alexander Hamilton.

It was such a peaceful place. The streets of Society Hill were closed from the avenues of commerce. People strolled through the neighborhoods during the springs and summers. The reliable tolling of a nearby church bell lent an additional feeling of security.

However, other parts of our lives were not so joyous and carefree. A year earlier many great men boldly signed the Declaration of Independence; as a result, our country struggled for autonomy.

Mr. Franklin stayed in France most of that year, attempting to negotiate an alliance with that great country. At home we waged bloody battle with the British, with conflicts at Lexington, Concord, Ticonderoga, Bunker Hill and Saratoga. The British had evacuated Boston. We residents of Philadelphia, because of British occupation, took temporary shelter in Allentown.

Indeed, during this time I learned that with adversity usually comes opportunity if I looked for it. Our soldiers required food, equipment and supplies, and I was in a position to provide these necessary items for them. After reassurement by our provisional government that I could best serve in this capacity rather than on the battle lines, I supplied goods for the army, at a fair profit, I must add.

Each year I plowed most of my earnings back into our business, increasing our inventory and facilities as well as our capital base. This afforded me the position to take advantage of other opportunities which arose as a result of the War of Independence. When the Articles of Peace were signed with Britain, our provisional government, in 1782, having no further need of the warehouses they erected during the conflict to hold supplies and equipment, put them up for public auction. I purchased them with the funds I had carefully guarded from my earnings.

This purchase launched me into whole new horizons of commerce and profitability. As a result, we created many new jobs for people, as well as offering a vastly expanded selection of goods and services to our patrons.

As my fortunes improved I began to be as concerned with retaining my worth as I was increasing it. I saw many otherwise intelligent people lose their hard-earned money by foolishly investing in unwise speculations. I had learned that years of struggle and saving could be wiped out by but a single unwise investment. So I had for some time deemed it wise to protect my assets at the same time as I increased my earnings.

Mr. Franklin previously shared with me the basis for his great wealth. Although accumulating money was never his goal, after establishing a profitable printing business in Philadelphia, and desirous of retiring, he turned it over to his foreman to manage. Continuing to receive one half of its profits each year, he established other partnerships from Newport and New York to Charleston. Each of the new shops gave him a part of their profits, installing competent, seasoned managers who had proven to him their business acumen and trustworthiness.

Money from these enterprises continually flowed in to build his sizable wealth. He explained to a friend one day that he had retired to enjoy the leisure to read, study and make experiments. In his own words he described his desire to, "converse at length with such ingenious and worthy men as are pleased to honor me with their friendship."

I learned many lessons from this great man.

Concerned with the security of my business, I accepted a policy from the Mutual Assurance Company which gave me comfort in knowing that if either my home or any of my stores and warehouses were destroyed, I would be reimbursed the necessary amount to rebuild. I felt this a very wise investment for my own peace of mind. I have often advised many people, of all levels of income, to do the same.

I predict the day will come when men commonly pay small sums to assurance companies for life protection. So that, should they experience a premature death or even a disability, their industry and frugality will be preserved and provision made for their survivors. I deem this an important and prudent action for everyone to take in order to enjoy great financial security and to pass on wealth to their descendants.

Shortly after the end of the Revolutionary War, I met with a few well-known men of the city, fellow members of the American Philosophical Association formed in 1743 by Mr. Franklin. We assembled regularly to discuss many issues of business and wealth and abundance. On this particular day our conversations centered around the ease of losing the wealth that we had worked so hard to accumulate.

As we talked, Walter Bradbury, one of the oldest in the group, who had been listening to the debate intently and with silence, interrupted with a remark that brought a hushed silence to the room.

"I have learned that it is more difficult," he said, "to keep your wealth than it is to earn it."

Glancing around the now silent room, he continued with a question, "Tell me, my friends, how many of you have lost money in unwise investments?"

We all raised our hands.

He smiled and said, "And so have I. I ask you all to reflect for a moment on your losses and tell me the reasons for them."

There was a quietude again as each of us looked back on what were in some ways painful experiences.

"A few years ago, I made a most extraordinary discovery," Mr. Bradbury went on when no one else spoke up. "I discovered that the losses of money I experienced were each connected with three causes. First of all, I lost money when I invested in a speculative venture, expecting quick, easy gains. Next, I lost money when I invested in an area in which I had no expertise. And thirdly, I lost money when I made investments that hinged on trusting other people's abilities or integrity.

"Now, how many of you share my experience with these three causes for unsuccessful investments?" he asked.

Dr. Arthur Brisbane, a smallish man in his late sixties, who was a prosperous physician and landowner immediately interjected. "In my younger years," he explained, "I was energetic and ambitious and impatient for success and prosperity. I met a man of great eloquence who was selling shares in a new organization which was to manufacture weapons, both rifles and handguns.

"He gave several of us a glowing forecast of how profitable this venture would be and how fortunate we were to be getting the advantage of an initial investment which would surely multiply in value many times over. He even showed us figures of expected earnings, which indicated that our original investment would increase itself ten times in the first two or three years. He then told us the names of some very reputable men in New York who were also planning to invest in the venture. My feeling, of course, was that if men of such stature were involved, this must surely be a sound opportunity."

"So what happened?" someone asked.

Frowning, Dr. Brisbane replied, "What happened was not good, I am afraid. When we pressed him for progress reports, the organizer told us that he was experiencing delays in assembling the necessary manufacturing equipment, though assuring us that everything was working out well.

"We noticed, in the meantime, that he was living quite well on our investment money. He purchased a grand home at Fifth and Locust Streets and entertained lavishly, even inviting many of his investors. At first, this impressed us and interested several other large investors. He talked of impending support from the likes of the Powels, the Willings, Dr. William Shippen and John Adams."

"And what happened?" I asked Dr. Brisbane.

Showing little emotion, he continued in a most reserved manner, sitting with one thin leg crossed over the other, starring down at his folded hands.

"Well, looking back, I see many signs of his chicanery, though his deception became obvious to us rather late. As I recall, after one particularly lavish splash at his home, he slipped quietly out of town, taking with him whatever money he still had."

I was a bit surprised that Dr. Brisbane used the word "splash." He seemed such a conservative person; words like that hardly sounded natural coming from his mouth. It revealed to me that he may have been just as wide-eyed, headstrong, and confident as we younger men were before he had experiences such as the one he described.

"I was so blinded by my own desire for quick gain," he concluded, "that I threw good sense to the wind."

Another gentleman spoke from the gathering. "You also learned another lesson, my friend: That just because you can trust the other investors, it's not also true of the person you trust to manage your investment."

Everyone nodded their heads in agreement. I assumed from their responses that they had all been guilty of that kind of misdirected trust.

Looking around the room I asked, "And what other lessons have you learned about wisely handling investment money?"

Charles Kent, owner of a well-established carriage-building business, a large, robust, jolly person, was first to answer my question. "A lesson I learned in a most unpleasant, painful way is to say 'no' to friends and relatives who, knowing that I have surplus funds, come to me in swarms asking me to finance their schemes.

"As I recall," he continued, "the first was my wife's brother, who, having had trouble holding a steady job, thought that the true path to riches was to open an inn. 'Everyone has to eat,' he explained to me. For the life of me, I failed to discover the wisdom of this statement, though he apparently recognized it himself. 'I will make this one profitable,' he continued confidently, 'and then I will open additional ones throughout the city.'

"I felt somewhat guilty for having money when he was not as fortunate, and not wanting to offend my wife and her relatives, I finally relented, to my folly. I felt from the beginning that I should not do it, but the pressures were more than I was willing to withstand at that young age. So I gave in to his requests.

"My brother-in-law had been a furniture maker. It...it all...well...now it all appears so simple. Why did I not ask myself and my brother-in-law, 'What experience does a furniture maker have running an inn?' Had I the experience I have now and had I asked myself that question, I probably would have answered, 'About as much chance as a politician achieving sainthood!'" He slapped his knee and roared with laughter.

We all laughed, and Charles Kent shifted in his chair, smiled broadly, and tamped his clay pipe.

"So what happened?" I asked.

"Well, predictably, he lost the money. It seems that he had underestimated the initial capital he would need which, as all of you know, is indeed a common mistake with people beginning a business."

We all nodded, for we had experienced this problem ourselves and had watched many others err in this same manner.

"Well"...Charles Kent went on, holding two fingers in the air. "In this instance I lost two ways! First, I lost the money I gave my brother-in-law. Then I further angered him, as well as the whole family, when I would not loan him the additional capital he needed to make up his shortfall. Soon most of the family blamed me for his failure."

"I, too, learned many years ago to never loan money to relatives," Walter Bradbury spoke up. "It rarely works out well."

Charles Kent responded with a joking manner, "And where were you when I needed you the most, Walter?"

We all laughed. Kent went on, "From this and a few other incidents, I have learned and have since followed a hard and fast rule to never loan money to people unless they have proven experience in the field in which they want to work. Looking back it, of course, made no sense to loan a furniture maker money to open an inn. Now I would only make a loan to someone who has successfully managed an inn, someone who knows the challenges involved and who has, by diligence and honesty, demonstrated his capability, his unquestionable expertise in that business or trade."

Charles Kent continued, looking at each of us in turn. "Another mistaken investment I see people make is when they place false trust in other people's abilities or integrity."

"Do you mean that we should never trust other people?" someone asked.

"Oh, no," Kent shot back. "What I mean is that we should carefully invest our money in enterprises in which we have some expertise or control, or where we are completely sure of the prudence of the individuals involved. I have often had very successful people come to me and ask, 'Where should I invest my surplus funds?' I always tell them, invest in yourself. Invest in the very things that you know and that have brought you success."

I immediately thought of Poor Richard's admonition: "He that by the plough would thrive, himself must either hold or drive."

After listening quietly to Charles Kent, Dr. Brisbane spoke up. "I have known physicians like myself, as well as other professionals, for instance, who, though very intelligent and expert in their professions, mistakenly came to the point of thinking they could make money in anything. So they backed speculative ventures about which they had no knowledge. They trusted other people's abilities. They were so confident in their own abilities that they thought everything they touched would be profitable. And, more often than not, they lost what they worked so hard to gain."

"Yes," Thomas McGregor agreed in his distinctive Scottish accent. "You are so correct, Dr. Brisbane."

Mr. McGregor cleared his throat and seemed to collect his thoughts before he spoke. "Tell me, my good laddies, all of us are reasonably successful, are we not? One would hardly be a member of this fine institution unless he had achieved a fair amount of wealth. We have all experienced various ups and downs in the business world."

Drawing a breath he continued, "Let me pose a question or two to this esteemed group. First, I repeat a question asked earlier: 'How many of you have lost money in enterprises before?'"

We all laughed and quickly raised our hands.

"All right. How many of you know others who have lost moncy they invested in various enterprises?"

We all started to talk at once, happy to move the focus from our own failures to those of others who had lost money in speculative ventures.

"Gentlemen!" McGregor said loudly as if to regain control of the gathering. "Now, I want you to think carefully before you answer this final question."

He paused to get our attention. "Excluding the money you have invested and earned in your own trade or profession, or others that were well managed—excluding these ways, how many of you would have been better off if you had never invested in any speculative venture, but had taken those surplus funds and placed them in a completely secure investment that paid a seemingly sparse six percent interest?

"Consider my question carefully before you answer, lads," McGregor emphasized with his colorful, clipped, controlled voice.

Each of us responded, all agreeing that except for rare instances we would have been much better off had we chosen a low interest, secure investment, rather than one which provided quick, easy returns.

"And how about your friends? How many of them do you think would also say that they, too, would have been better off to have chosen a course of safety? Are there any exceptions among them?"

No one's hand went up. Mr. McGregor's wise observations of other peoples' investment habits led me to understand the point he was making.

I thought about his point, then and often since. Yes, I knew of one or two people who had benefited from what seemed to be lucky ventures. Yes, I even knew some people who, because of timing or luck, became wealthy through what seemed to me to be risky investments. But try as I might, I could not think of very many.

The longer I live, the more convinced I become that those who invest in enterprises other than their own would be far better off, over the length of their days, if they stayed with secured investments with a guaranteed rate of return. Yes, no matter how small the rate of return, by not losing their seed money, eventually they would fare better.

As I have reflected on this belief I have been aware of people who have funds to invest, but who do not have sufficient funds or the desire to purchase a business. Mr. Franklin and I have often talked about the formation of a mutual holding company that would wisely and carefully invest people's savings in several successful businesses.

It has been our observation that this would provide both opportunity and safety for their investment, while it is being managed by competent, prudent people, skilled in the art of business and enterprise. This would allow individuals to benefit from successful businesses while lessening their personal risks.

Still another mistake I have noticed is that of investing in speculative ventures with borrowed money. I advise young people to never borrow money that they intend to put at risk. Now, does that mean that I say never risk? No! We all run risks and will continue to do so, even as we attempt to minimize them. What I mean is, do not go into debt in order to invest in risky ventures.

Mr. Franklin once said, through the pen of Poor Richard, "Vessels large may venture more, but little boats should keep near shore."

Yes, I know, we can all point to individuals who risked everything only to enjoy a high return overnight. Yes, of course, there are a few people like that. But how many more borrowed money to put into risky investments, only to learn the pinch of debt that led to a permanent state of poverty? You do not hear much of those.

My advice is to risk what you can afford to risk. If you cannot afford to lose your investment, do not put it where there is a chance of losing it.

Wise people know that money invested which yields only small returns, if adhered to over the years, will guarantee wealth. It will also assure the retention of your capital. As Poor Richard wrote, "Light gains grow into heavy purses." Also, "Little strokes fell great oaks", and "Make haste slowly."

Anyone can become wealthy, if beginning when they are young, they will form the habit of investing where there is safety. Then as their investment yields returns, faithfully reinvesting them, also. The compounding nature of this habit, regardless of how small the amounts, will surely grow into significant sums eventually.

Although I myself am a hopeful optimist, I always advise those who seek my advice about investing, "If you invest in risky, speculative enterprises, be prepared to lose your money because the chances are great that you will."

Yes, after listening for scores of years to many men wise in the handling of money and reflecting on my own experiences, my advice is to invest where you will enjoy the greatest safety.

For all the people I encounter who make unwise decisions about investing their money in speculative ventures, I only wish they could have heard the advice of Mr. Kent, Dr. Brisbane, Mr. McGregor and others that evening at the American Philosophical Society.

Many people have profited from the wisdom of those men who were so skilled at the handling of money.

THE SIXTH LAW OF WEALTH AND ABUNDANCE

INVEST WITH THE GREATEST PRUDENCE AND SAFETY

Invest your money in yourself, after you have developed experienced skills. Avoid speculative ventures where you expect quick, easy returns. Keep your money away from ventures where you have no experience, unless you have people you can completely trust who do have the experience. Diligently protect yourself from the risks that life often brings, insuring yourself and your properties from unwelcomed loss. Give no one control of your funds who has not demonstrated unquestionable integrity and good financial judgment. Be satisfied with lower returns where you can enjoy the reasonable safety of your principal. Be watchful, remembering that it is thrice as difficult to keep what you have than to first earn it.

Chapter 7

The Seventh Law of Wealth and Abundance

BORROW ONLY WHAT YOU HAVE THE ABILITY TO REPAY

Seventeen hundred and eighty-three was one of those years that stand out in the memories of the people of this great nation. It was the year the definitive Treaty of Peace was proclaimed, coming one year after the preliminary Articles of Peace, signed with Britain. The war had been a terrible experience, many lives were lost and great numbers of people were separated from their roots in England.

Dr. Franklin, as the French press began to call him a few years ago, had been appointed Minister to the French court, and he spent considerable time in that country. He resigned that post in 1781 and was appointed to the peace commission here in our country. His life was full and rich. His good wife Deborah had passed from this life in 1774. The French press reported his friendship with Lady Helvetius, creating quite a story that she had rejected his proposal of marriage shortly before he resigned his commission there in France.

Rebecca, Benjamin and I had lived in our wonderful home on Walnut Street for six years by then. What a marvelous feeling it was to stand in our entry and watch the carriages slowly come up the road into the drive, finally stopping in front of our home where their passengers joined us on many occasions. Many leaders of our city, as well as our country, have graced our home with their presence.

Spring was always Rebecca's favorite time of year. She loved the brilliant tulips with their vivid red, yellow and lilac blooms, as she did the beautiful hyacinths that edged our circular drive. My heart always burst with happiness as I saw Rebecca grace our home with her beauty and vibrant spirit. As we prayed together in the evenings we were constantly moved by the richness of the blessings that the Creator had showered upon us. Often it seemed like possibly it was all a dream, a fantasy.

As I reflect back on my years and write this little book, dear reader, my intent is to share the lessons of life I have learned with those who sincerely want to travel the road to wealth. To give those of you who are intent on improving your lots in life a simple guide for enjoying greater prosperity.

It strikes me that few people whose possessions grow and multiply escape the use of credit. I have also noticed that more people get into financial trouble because of debt than any other reason. As I look back through the years I can name person after person who reached a state of poverty because they had borrowed heavily, only to meet some adversity or bad luck which made them unable to meet their obligations. Most could have survived the adversity itself had they not had the added burden of paying back past principal and accumulated interest.

I have also observed that, given time, few people escape adversities. Life brings with it ups and downs, good times and bad times, periods when everything seems to bless us and other periods when good fortune apparently refrains its visits upon us. Yes, it's true that given enough time, no one escapes the ravaging pains of adversity. I have personally weathered the storms of many buffeting experiences.

I discussed the subject of credit on several occasions with Dr. Franklin. He was such a famous person the last few years of his life, having spent much time in the courts of France, that I only enjoyed short amounts of time with him during his last years in Philadelphia. He was pleased at the prosperity which I enjoyed. I often thanked him, face to face as well as in notes and letters, to which his response was always the same. He smiled as he turned and looked down modestly, then he raised his twinkling eyes to mine and said, "The greatest gift of friendship, Andrew, is the gift of an idea. The greatest response to a gift is to pass it on to another."

When he knew his words had sunk in, he always added enthusiastically, "And the greatest way to show appreciation for a gift is to use it and then pass it on to another deserving person! But always remember, Andrew," he would continue as he raised his left index finger in the air for emphasis, "he who will not be counseled, cannot be helped. And remember, too, that a good example is the best sermon!" Then he often quoted his favorite Proverb from King Solomon, "A wise man will hear and increase learning."

What a fascinating man Dr. Franklin was. I owe so much to him. When I was with him I always felt that he was in the very center of history in the making. Little did I know then how prophetic this feeling was.

He had so many wise sayings that he had first put into the words of his fictitious character Richard Saunders, or as the world knew him, Poor Richard. I watched many people listen to his wise words only to see most pass them off as the babblings of someone who simply wanted to hear himself talk. He not only believed his wisdom to be the way to more prosperous living, but he was a practitioner of it. It was here I learned that wise people will receive counsel, but foolish people will either see no value in or shun good advice.

Dr. Franklin found in me a person who was not only burning to learn from his wisdom, but also one who listened and applied his advice. Looking back now, I see that this was a fact in which he took confidence, as he would not have taken his valuable time to instruct and counsel me had he not detected this hunger in me.

I have learned a lesson, over and over, that wise people are usually willing to invest their time and wisdom in people who genuinely want to learn. My appreciation to this great man was best expressed by my commitment to him to pass on to others what he had taught me. This is a promise that I have worked most persistently in carrying out.

Once, years ago, right after I acquired my first mercantile store from Mrs. Whitworth, Dr. Franklin said to me, "Andrew, if you truly intend to increase your wealth, you must learn the wise use of credit. Credit can be one of your best business tools, or it can surely drag you down into the mire of poverty. Always remember that a good paymaster is lord of another man's purse. Another good lesson I have learned," he often said to me, always with a slight grin, "is that creditors have better memories than debtors. When you run into debt, you give another man power over your liberty, because the borrower is often a slave to the lender."

I still remember the time that Dr. Franklin asked me, "Have you ever suffered the pains of owing money which you found difficult to repay?"

My answer was not long in forthcoming. "Yes, sir, I have certainly had that problem, and a painful and humbling memory it is."

"Would you tell me of an instance when this happened?" he asked.

For a moment I searched my mind. "Well, I remember, some years ago, a time when Rebecca became very ill. The nature of her illness was such that I became greatly melancholy. There were many expenses associated with her condition, far beyond my ability to handle at that time. I still remember spending numerous sleepless nights turning and twisting, wrestling with this problem, attempting to find a solution. "How could I settle my accounts on but a clerk's pay?" I asked myself this question again and again during that time. Of course my major concern was for Rebecca's health, but still I worried about ending up in a debtor's court. I realize now that because so many pressures and anxieties were upon me, my ability to think clearly had completely left me."

"Pray tell me what happened?" Dr. Franklin asked.

"Well, an acquaintance employed at the shop near our store told me of a certain man here in Philadelphia who loaned money to those who needed it badly. 'But I have nothing to offer as collateral,'" I told him.

"'Oh, you'll need no security,'" he said to me. "'This man is eager to help those who cannot go to a banker.'"

"'But I do not understand,'" I said. "'Why would he take a risk on me when he knows nothing about me or my financial situation?'"

"Oh, he will charge you a little more interest than you would pay a banker, for sure, but at least your money problems will be solved," this acquaintance assured me.

"I should have known that this sounded too good to be true. A man who would lend me all the money I needed without any collateral? But I was desperate to do whatever it took to restore Rebecca's health and establish order in our household once again. So I went to see the man, and I will admit that I felt very strange from the moment I arrived. The man was friendly enough, but, there was a coldness in his eyes that made me feel uneasy. I also noticed something in his handshake that caused me to shiver with fear. There was a lack of any grip. However, I did not listen to these instinctive warnings, and the transaction was as quick and easy as my acquaintance promised it would be. I had only to sign a document and very soon I left with the money I needed.

"For a brief period I felt relieved that my immediate problem was solved. Soon, however, the cold man demanded payment which far exceeded what the normal rates of interest were at the time or what I had expected from our agreement."

"What did you do?"

"Well, at first I protested, to which he produced the document I had signed, and I realized that, in my anxiety, I had signed it without thoroughly reading it or understanding his interpretation of its words. At first I argued with him, explaining to him my understanding of the agreement and how it was different from what I now saw that the document said."

"And how did he reply to that?"

"Very harshly, sir. In fact, he threatened to have me sent to debtor's prison and to expose me to my employer."

"And so what happened?"

"Well, somehow I was able to satisfy his demands. It took almost two years to complete the payments, and I must have paid him back three times as much as I borrowed.

"Sir, aside from sharing this experience with Rebecca after her illness had passed, I have never told anyone else about this. But, looking back, I suppose that although the cost was extremely high, it was worth the lesson I learned. It was certainly worth the restoration of Rebecca's health."

"When you run into debt, you give someone else the power over your liberty," Dr. Franklin repeated seriously.

"Yes, sir," I nodded. "I well appreciate the wisdom in those words."

"That reminds me," he said, a smile coming to his face, "of what that paragon of wisdom Poor Richard once wrote, 'When you make your bargain, you may, perhaps, think little of payment; but creditors have better memories than debtors.'"

He chuckled with twinkling eyes as he further observed, "Creditors are a superstitious sect, being great observers of set days and times!"

He went on. "Over the years I have observed the habits of many people, particularly as they have incurred debts. Now, please, do not misunderstand me. Credit, if properly used, is an honorable thing; in fact, governments and enterprises cannot function without credit, and the proper use of it creates opportunity and prosperity. It is, in fact, necessary for most businesses if they want to function properly. For well-managed businesses and people who can earn ten to twelve percent on their invested capital, it is a wise practice to purchase the use of money for, say, six percent. But it is the misuse of borrowed money which enslaves and drags people down into poverty. Through unwise management and reckless speculation, I have seen many upstanding citizens reduced to paupers and forced to borrow from people who were base and immoral, but who, through frugality, had stored away surpluses. Their brutish ways were repulsive to the genteel borrowers, but the borrowers bent their knees and condescended to them.

"Andrew, if you want to know the value of money," Dr. Franklin continued, "go and try to borrow some, for, as Poor Richard said, 'He who goes a borrowing, goes a sorrowing!' Another common thing that happens to the borrower is that suddenly the days seem to have wings and they swiftly speed by. In fact, when borrowed money is coming due, time flies more rapidly than ever before! Terms which at first seemed so reasonable and manageable, suddenly loom before a man. Again to quote Poor Richard, 'Those have a short Lent who owe money to be paid by Easter!'"

Dr. Franklin taught me many good practices regarding credit, and I have made many observations myself. I have noticed, for instance, that the inability to pay one's debts causes heretofore honest men to temporarily resort to dishonesty, with the telling of falsehoods or half-truths in an attempt to deal with their immediate problems. When they cannot pay on time, they are ashamed to face their creditors. They dread meeting them on the streets, they make pitiful excuses when questioned, and, by degrees, compromise their integrity. Their work suffers and they often drift from place to place. It was again Poor Richard who wrote, "The second vice is lying, the first is running in debt! Lying rides on debt's back." Yes, I have observed that when driven to the wall by failing circumstances, a person's integrity often diminishes.

So, wise people are careful in how they use credit. They realize that if they are to achieve the measure of prosperity of which they are capable, they will need to learn the wise use of it.

I have often thought of another personal experience Dr. Franklin related to me years ago. He told me how, as a young tradesman, he opened a little stationer's shop. He explained how he stocked blanks of all sorts: like paper, parchment, Chapman's books and other items.

"I began gradually to pay off the debt I was under for the printing house," he explained. "In order to secure my credit and character as a tradesman, I took care not only to be industrious and frugal, but also avoided all appearances to the contrary. I dressed plainly; I was seen at no places of idle diversion. My creditors could hear the sound of my presses early in the morning as they passed by on their way to work; they could also see a light in my shop when they were going to their homes in the evening.

"I learned that a good paymaster is lord of another man's purse. He that is known to pay punctually and exactly on the time he promises, may at any time and on any occasion raise all the money his friends can spare. After industry and frugality, nothing contributes more to the success of a young man in the world than punctuality and justice in all his dealings. Therefore, never keep borrowed money an hour beyond the time you promised, lest a disappointment shut up your friend's purse forever."

Well, as I mentioned I was only a young man then. I still remember replying, "Sir, you are a wise man, full of years, and I am but a young lad whose only wealth is his eagerness to learn."

Dr. Franklin smiled and said, "Then listen carefully, my young friend, because what I tell you, if understood and practiced, can make you the master of much wealth. The most trifling actions that affect a man's credit are to be regarded. The sound of your hammer heard by a creditor at five in the morning or nine at night makes him easy to deal with six months longer. But if he sees you at a billiard table or hears your voice at a tavern when you should be at work, he will send for money the next day."

Concluding the subject, he said, "It shows, besides, that you are mindful of what you owe. It also makes you appear a careful and honest man, and it still increases your credit."

His words seemed so simple and obvious that I almost responded, "Oh, I already know that!" But before I spoke out I reminded myself that while I might have known this wisdom, I was not then practicing it.

A mistake I have seen many people make is to be too optimistic, when borrowing, about their ability to repay. I have especially noticed this trait in people who have a high degree of self confidence. They think they can do anything, so they run risks which are foolish. They do not allow for unforeseen ill circumstances that can come into one's life without warning. When unpleasant circumstances do come, they are unprepared to deal with them. First, they avoid their creditors, often thinking up excuses and promises that have little chance of proving out. Then, when it gets too late for excuses and desperate promises, they, being in such dire situations, have little chance to work out their problems.

I learned early in my business life to keep my creditors informed of my current affairs, to furnish them with plenty of information as to my financial condition. I discovered that my steadfastness in doing this helped me develop their trust and maintain their respect. I learned, too, that when creditors trust and respect you they will more eagerly work with you when adversity does strike, as it does at some point in every person's life.

Another lesson I learned from experience is that even a small amount, regularly paid, not only kept my creditors happy, but it put me in good standing with them. When they saw my persistence and diligence in paying them, they gladly opened their purses to me in future days. I discovered, too, that the use of money is the main advantage of having money. For six pence a year, I could have the use of one hundred pence. From this, I realized that if I took that one hundred pence and used it to earn ten, this justified the borrowing. Once I had proven I could show this kind of profit in my expanding mercantile business, I had large sums of money available to me. But regardless of the sum, the principle was the same: It is only wise to borrow money when you can use it to earn more than its cost.

Well, dear reader, these are my humble comments on the practice of the proper handling of credit. Through the years I have witnessed that these principles are commonly violated by many people, which to me explains why so few people enjoy wealth.

Yes, people who prosper are ones who handle their credit wisely, ones who have developed promptness and diligence in their dealings with creditors.

You may avoid many failures and heartaches by observing this seventh law of wealth and abundance: *Borrow only what you have the ability to repay.*

The Seventh Law of Wealth and Abundance

BORROW ONLY WHAT YOU HAVE THE ABILITY TO REPAY

Credit can be one of your most important business tools, or it can drag you down into the mire of poverty. The use of credit is an honorable activity for those knowledgeable in the laws of it. Do not make debts that strain your future or in which repayment depends on miracles. Keep your creditors well informed. Should you have current or past-due debt, go to your creditors and ask to work out a systematic plan. They will be impressed with your honesty and steadiness, even though you consistently pay back only small payments. Small payments, regularly made, will bring you their everlasting respect. Few things will block your road to wealth and abundance as will unwise borrowing.

Chapter 8

THE EIGHTH LAW OF WEALTH AND ABUNDANCE

ESTABLISH GOOD HABITS AND THEY WILL ESTABLISH YOU

Only when you can manage yourself will you be entrusted with money to manage.

In my discussions of wealth and abundance with the young people I tutor, I often hear the question, "Why are not more people successful?" My answer to this query is usually quite simple. Unfortunately most people who ask are not satisfied with my reply but appear disappointed and turn away. Often they have not heard what they wanted to hear.

Still others, upon hearing my words, scowl at me as if I were withholding the real truth. Others nod and smile and go their own way, certain never to act upon my advice. A few heed my advice, soaking up what I have learned from experience. These are the few with whom I then choose to invest my time.

"Why are not more people successful?" The answer can be summed up in this simple truth: *Establish good habits and they will establish you.* It is true that most of us are the creatures of our habits. Wise people, recognizing this, diligently work to establish habits that will yield the successful results they desire.

"Diligence is the mother of good luck" was the oft-quoted advice of Poor Richard which Dr. Franklin loved to say to young people, smiling to himself as he talked through the wise man of his own invention.

His message could be summed up as saying that people's wealth and outer circumstances are the natural results of their thoughts, habits, and character. It disturbed him no little when so few people caught his true meaning. To him it was as clear and logical as the growth of a seedling. "Establish good habits and they will establish you," he often reminded people.

One story he loved to tell, one of his own invention, of course, was about a man who stopped his horse one day and listened to people conversing about the difficulties of the times. Amongst them was a plain old man with white locks. "'Pray, what think you of the times?' the people asked this old man. 'Will not these heavy taxes quite ruin the country? How shall we be ever able to pay them? What would you advise us to do?'

"'Friends,' said he, 'and neighbors, the taxes are indeed heavy, and if those laid on by the government were the only ones we had to pay, we might more easily discharge them; but we have many others, and much more grievous ones to some of us. We are taxed twice as much by our idleness, three times as much by our pride, and four times as much by our folly, and from these taxes commissioners cannot ease or deliver us by allowing an abatement.'"

His eyes gleamed as he shared this tale, looking penetratingly into the eyes of his listeners as if to detect their comprehension.

As he reflected upon how people reacted to his advice on wealth and prosperity, Franklin often said, "We may give good advice, but we cannot give conduct."

I heard his advice and made a pledge to myself, and to him, that I would exercise diligence in not only hearing his words, but also applying them to my daily affairs. And as I have mentioned to you before, dear reader, I have discovered that by passing along his wisdom to others I increased it by giving it away. This way I learn thrice: Once in the hearing, once in the practice, and once in the sharing with others.

I learned this profound truth years ago as I heard, practiced, and related to others the wisdom of Dr. Franklin. Once, as he had on several occasions, he sent me a note requesting my presence in his home to see one of his new inventions. What an active mind he possessed. He continually plunged into unknown areas, never satisfied with things as they were. I marveled at the number of activities he could work into his days and nights. Even in the midst of the great conflict with England, as he wrestled with all the problems of that time and helped to make decisions that would surely shape the world's direction, he still allowed his active mind to seek its directions.

On one particular occasion I had not seen him for several months, as he had just returned from France. When I arrived at his home, he greeted me, just as jovial as always. Dispensing with idle chatter, he said to me, "Andrew, come with me."

Thereupon he took my arm and ushered me to a room at the rear of the house. Opening the door, he proudly displayed another of his strange-looking contraptions, this time a rather large wooden tub, at least six feet in diameter, filled with steaming water.

"What is it?" I asked.

He replied with a chuckle, "It is a device to make old, tired bones feel young again.

"Come, let me show you."

He pointed to a metal tank in the room's small fireplace. "That tank, my friend, is filled with water. When it is heated, it runs down this pipe and into the wooden tub. After the nice, warm, revitalizing bath, one need only pull the plug in the outlet in the bottom and the water runs out again."

I watched Dr. Franklin's eyes twinkle as he showed off his latest invention with the enthusiasm of a small child. I marveled that although he had just spent months in France negotiating with the most powerful leaders in the world, a simple, though brilliant, invention could fill him with joy. This incredible range of interests was one thing I loved about this man and why the memories of the moments I spent with him are still so precious to me.

As I examined the source of his excitement, he suddenly could contain himself no longer. "Take off your clothes, Andrew, and I will share with you the greatest feeling of relaxation that you have ever known."

"Take off my clothes?" I knew not whether he was serious or how I should react.

"Yes," he exclaimed, pointing to my clothing, "take off your clothes." And he began unbuttoning his own shirt, then, right there in front of me, stripped off all his clothes, stepped onto the platform that encircled the wooden tub and gleefully entered the steaming water.

"Come on in, Andrew" he urged.

It was clear that he would not be satisfied until I joined him. As I tentatively stuck one foot into the hot water, he roared, "Plunge yourself in, Andrew. Timid souls never conquer strong foes!"

So I dropped my whole body into the steaming, soothing water and felt the wonders of the heat encircle me. Through the steam I looked at Dr. Franklin, who had closed his eyes and was smiling peacefully. He seemed to have cleansed his mind of all thought except that of this relaxed sensation.

"I saw something like this in Paris," he explained when he came back to reality enough to speak. "I think they got the idea from the Chinese. I have not had the courage to tell many people about it. I tried to get Alexander Hamilton into it just the other day, but the idea offended his dignity, I think."

A most mischievous look came over his face. Grinning broadly, he went on, "I suppose he was afraid that his political friends would think that plopping into a tub full of hot water with an old, naked, fat man would not do his public image any good." He roared with laughter at the thought, slapping the water and sending wet rivulets spluttering onto the floor.

"Sir," I asked with a teasing tone, catching his mischievous spirit, "what would the ladies from Paris think if they saw you now?"

He roared even louder and once again slapped the water, and his rotund, pink body churned the water as he thoroughly enjoyed the moment. "Madam Helvetius would once again rejoice at rejecting my proposal of marriage," he slyly chirped.

"And what would Rebecca think if she saw you here with this old fat man?" he retorted.

"She would no doubt be quite envious, sir, for she would see that this is one of the most relaxing things that I have ever done."

Breathing deeply, I gave myself over to sensation and soon forgot the ridiculousness of the scene. I felt my stresses and fatigue floating out into the water. For a few minutes we were both silent, lost in our own thoughts and feelings.

Later, as we toweled off and dressed, the great man said to me, "Andrew, knowing you has been a most rewarding and refreshing experience. You have truly learned well. I watched the seeds of knowledge enter you, take root, grow and multiply. I commend you for your great achievement."

"Thank you, sir. I can never fully express how much your words of wisdom have helped me, nor can I ever repay you."

"Repay me?" he responded. "Of course you can repay me! And you must! I expect it. You can repay me by passing on to others the ideas I have given you. Ideas to wise people are worth more than gold. Of course," he continued, "ideas to foolish people are worth nothing. However, remember that the greatest gift you can give to another is the gift of an idea."

He said this as he buttoned his shirt cuffs and pulled a heavy sweater over his head.

"Andrew," he went on, motioning for me to follow him into his study. "There's a very special idea that I want to share with you tonight. It is one that you can use for as long as you live. No matter how successful you become you will refer to this simple idea each day of your life. You may also," he added as if an afterthought, "give it to other people who sincerely want to learn."

Motioning for me to be seated, he opened a drawer in his mahogany secretary and retrieved a small memorandum book. For a moment he flipped through its worn pages.

"Years ago...ah, it was near the year 1743, I believe," he continued. "I decided that I wished to live without committing any fault at any time. But as I pursued this endeavor, I soon found it was a task more difficult than I had first imagined it would be. While I employed care in guarding against one fault, I was often surprised by my laxity in another. I learned from this experience that contrary habits must be broken and good ones acquired. To do this I conceived a bold and arduous plan to reach moral perfection."

Then Mr. Franklin laid out his plan. He told me that he had made a list of the thirteen virtues or traits in which he wished to excel. The virtues were temperance, silence, order, resolution, frugality, industry, sincerity, justice, moderation, tranquility, cleanliness, chastity, and humility.

"I gauged that it would be well not to distract my attention by attempting to achieve the whole list at once, but to focus on one of them at a time, and to pursue that virtue until it became a habit. To keep track of my progress I made a little book in which I ruled each page with red ink so as to have seven columns, one for each day of the week, marking each column with a letter signifying that day. I crossed these columns with thirteen red lines, marking the beginning of each line with the first letter of one of the virtues, on which line and in its proper column I might mark a little black spot every fault I found upon examination to have been committed respecting that virtue upon that day.

"With this system I determined to give a week's strict attention to each virtue successively, thus developing fixed habits within myself. It would take me thirteen weeks to work through all the virtues, which I could do four times a year."

That evening Dr. Franklin described in detail this system that had been of great value to him over the years. By concentrating his efforts on one virtue at a time, he said, he more nearly mastered them all. He explained how he strictly evaluated his performance each day and recorded his accomplishments and failures in the little book. He carried it with him always, and this self-evaluation helped him develop into habits the virtues he desired.

In the days that followed I thought much of Dr. Franklin's pursuit of virtues and character traits and the system he had employed to achieve his goal of virtuous habits. I decided I would do the same exercise. So I obtained a small notebook, and for several days I carried it in my coat pocket.

Whenever they came to me, I wrote down the personal traits, attitudes and habits I wanted to develop. I added and deleted traits until, within a fortnight, I had selected thirteen that seemed to be ones I most needed.

I selected these traits:

1. Honor the Creator daily.
2. Demonstrate a thankful spirit.
3. Show forgiveness and humility towards others.
4. Apply courtesy in all transactions.
5. Be diligent in daily affairs.
6. Practice temperance in food and drink.
7. Use wisdom in the handling of money.
8. Encourage others around me.
9. Balance work and recreation.
10. Manage time well.
11. Contribute to the welfare of others.
12. Spend study and planning time daily.
13. Listen to others without judgment or bias.

Like Mr. Franklin, I designed a small memorandum book and allotted a separate page to each of these traits. I ruled seven columns to the right of each trait and marked each column with a letter symbolizing a day of the week.

I began to concentrate all my efforts on one trait for one full week. At the end of each day I examined my performance of that trait, thinking how I had applied it and also how I could have applied it better in more situations. I noted my accomplishments and failures in the notebook, and then I determined a score for my efforts, using the numbers one through ten—one being "very poor" or "no attention paid to that trait" while ten indicated "excellent in application."

This daily practice caused me to be more observant of other people's actions as well as my own. It helped me to see the evidence of these noble character traits in the success of others. I also noticed the lack of these traits in unsuccessful people. I began to see that some people attempted to cut corners, not valuing these success characteristics. I also witnessed the values of other people, and how these provided them with internal anchors and moral compasses that helped them steer through life's storms. I met many people who scoffed at the traits I pursued, considering them child's play or nice things to talk about, but not serious traits to adopt in their everyday lives. I, in time, observed that these people, while seeking success, most often found it elusive and impossible to achieve.

What a tragedy, I told myself many times, the traits that bring success are so simple they are hidden from most people who unfortunately look in the wrong places. Although I had previously understood the importance of habits in my life, this experience helped me to perceive their power more deeply. I began to see that my daily, unconscious practices influence my success more than almost anything else. In fact, I have observed that events which appear to be good fortune or luck are but the result of good habits that have been well formed as part of a person's character.

Dr. Franklin told me, late in his life, after scoring himself in his thirteen areas time and again, that at first he thought this system would one day help him reach moral perfection. But with the years, he discovered that, for mortals, perfection is not to be attained. He explained, "I realized that the more I developed in one area, the more room for growth I discovered in another. I also noticed that frequent were the times when I caught myself slipping back in one or more areas. The more satisfied I became with myself, the more humility I lost! And...so it went."

Pausing and taking a deep breath he went on, "Eventually I came to terms with this nagging paradox and concluded that it is not within man's possibilities to achieve moral perfection in this life, that to expect perfection is folly. Upon discovering this, I felt cheated for all the effort I had expended. This frustration lasted for a while until I concluded that perfection is withheld from man until the next life."

Staring into space, his left foot propped on a small stool, he reminisced. "To allow man to even approach perfection in this life would indeed rob him of that one great hope of being transformed into the likeness of the Almighty. Andrew, I have never been much of a religious man. To me, most of man's religion creates more problems, fears, and uncertainties than it solves. It gives people a platform upon which to espouse any of their thousands of self-serving beliefs."

I listened carefully to him, never having heard him speak in terms like this.

"But the older I become, the more I believe in a divine Creator. If not a sparrow can fall to the ground without His knowledge, then how can each of us skip through life without His daily notice?"

We were both quiet for a few moments.

I still remember the warm feelings of that wonderful evening, although many years have passed since then. The lessons I learned were many. Mainly I learned that I am the creature of the sum of my habits; my habits being those actions I do without conscious thought. It was at this point I discovered a most simple truth: Habits are best formed by consciously practicing an action daily. From this period of repeated daily attention to the action, a habit is formed. It then can serve us as a silent force for years to come.

Since that night I have shared this technique of personal improvement with many people. I have suggested they begin by deciding upon the traits they want to internalize as habits, then concentrate on them one at a time. Once these good habits are instituted, they then appear when needed as unconscious behaviors and responses. Over and over I have seen this simple yet profound truth help carry people to new heights of prosperity and good fortune.

The truth is simply this: *Establish good habits and they will establish you.*

The Eighth Law of Wealth and Abundance

ESTABLISH GOOD HABITS AND THEY WILL ESTABLISH YOU

Observe successful people and seek their advice as to the personal qualities that brought them success. Define your own list of thirteen traits. Think of attitudes, habits or traits that will enhance your own prosperity. Write down these thirteen traits in a booklet, on a folded sheet of paper, or on a card. Draw seven columns to the right of each trait and mark each one with a letter for a day of the week. Focus your attention on one trait for a week. Note your failures and accomplishments, and grade yourself on your daily performance. Go to the next trait for a week, until you have done all thirteen. Then start over with your first one for thirteen weeks, and continue for several quarters. As your needs change, change your list of desired traits. Soon you will feel surges of growth in yourself and your outer success will more naturally follow.

Chapter 9

THE NINTH LAW OF WEALTH AND ABUNDANCE

CHOOSE TO ASSOCIATE WITH WISE, SUCCESSFUL PEOPLE

You will usually grow to the level of those with whom you choose to associate.

I have often observed that people, being given the power of choice by their Creator, meet many junctures that cause them to choose the roads they take in life. Some choose roads that lead to prosperity and abundance; others select paths that lead to poverty and want.

While no one would consciously choose poverty and want, they often unconsciously select it by the directions in which they take their lives and the choices they make.

In the last chapter I shared with you the power of personal habits and character traits in influencing success and financial security. I suggested that you choose thirteen traits that you want to establish within your own personal behavior that will then lead you to high levels of achievement and fulfillment. Whether or not you took action and did this was, of course, a choice you made.

Another choice you will either consciously or unconsciously make is that of the people with whom you associate. Few choices will influence your future more than this decision. One of the most profound truths I have learned is that people will rise or fall to the level of those with whom they choose to associate. It has become extremely clear to me over the years that the choice of friends and associates predetermines much of people's success and achievement. I learned this great lesson first from Dr. Franklin. I have spent the rest of my life learning more about it. My own prosperity, influenced by this great man, gives testimony to this principle.

In our discussions, Dr. Franklin often said these intriguing words: "Associate with people who enjoy the measure of prosperity that you would like to enjoy." This advice arrested my attention to no small degree. Once he paused after saying this, looked at me with his penetrating eyes, then continued. "It is a truth well worth remembering, my friend, that if you associate with people who enjoy the measure of prosperity you would like to enjoy, you will soon enjoy that level of prosperity yourself."

"But, sir," I argued, "Why would someone more successful than me want to spend time with me?"

"Good question," he chuckled. "And my answer is that they might not want to spend time with you if they perceive that doing so is a waste of their own time. But should they think that the time they spend with you is a good investment, then they might view it as a positive way to invest it. Wise people usually have time to help those who sincerely want to learn."

Over the years I have spent many hours thinking about these and other words I heard from this great man. He, himself, validated his own advice. It was he, the most famous man in the world, who gave so much of himself to others. Why, the hours he allowed me to spend with him over the years are far too numerous to count.

Very comfortable with himself, his modesty would not allow him to admit that his lofty position in the world could lift those of us whom he mentored up to a higher level than we would otherwise experience. I am quite certain though, that he was well aware that it did.

I have often noticed, over the years, that people's achievements are indeed significantly influenced by others with whom they associate. Some of the people who surround and influence us are there by our selection. We choose them. These would be people like friends, acquaintances, business associates. Others are in our lives not because of our selection. We do not choose them; they are just there. These are people like family members. Almost everyone with whom we associate influences us, either negatively or positively.

Some people have as their objective to build us up, while others want to keep us pressed down. Those who press us down often do so by trying to control us and keep us from growing above them. Those who build us up find joy in seeing us grow and prosper, even beyond the level of achievement they, themselves, enjoy.

Wise people recognize and understand the differences between people who will nurture them and those who will not and take advantage of this knowledge. They consciously surround themselves with people who are supportive of them. They avoid or protect themselves from people who would inhibit their growth. Regarding this subject, Poor Richard had a most appropriate statement that he often printed in his almanacks. He wrote, "He who lies down with dogs, rises up with fleas." I have repeated the truth many times in a bit less colorful way: "He who associates with prosperous people will also know prosperity."

Dr. Franklin explained that he realized this while still quite young. In the autumn of 1727, he organized a group of men, called the Junto, who met on Friday evenings. In his own words, the group was, "A club formed by my ingenious acquaintances for mutual improvement." Franklin found the idea in the book *Essays to Do Good*, written by Cotton Mather, a Puritan minister. While the minister's goal was to form such a group to promote religion and morality, Franklin, though not an outwardly religious man, immediately recognized the significance of the exercise. He formed the club for the mutual betterment of its members and of the city and colony in which they lived.

As Dr. Franklin expected, the group's members soon began to rise to positions of power and influence in Philadelphia. Within a few short years, many of them were exerting extremely strong political influence in the city and colony.

Many good public works arose from the Junto. Its initial project was to form the first subscription library in North America, an idea that came to the group shortly after it was formed, when the members agreed that it would be beneficial to pool their books in a common place. They all brought their books to the room they had rented for their weekly meetings. Each member was then at liberty to borrow a book to take home to read at leisure.

As he told me this story years ago, Dr. Franklin further explained: "Finding the advantage of this little collection, I proposed to render the benefit from books more common by commencing a Public Subscription Library. I drew a sketch of the plan and articulated the rules that would be necessary, and got a skillful conveyancer, Mr. Charles Brockden, to put the whole in terms of *Articles of Agreement* to be subscribed. Each subscriber would agree to pay a certain sum down for the purchase of books and an annual contribution for increasing them.

"So few were the readers at that time in Philadelphia, and the majority of us poor, that I was not able, despite great industry, to find more than fifty persons, mostly tradesmen, willing to put down for this purpose forty shillings each and ten shillings per annum. The books were imported. The library was open one day in the week for lending to the subscribers, on their promissory notes to pay double the value if not duly returned.

"The institution soon manifested its utility and was imitated by other towns and provinces. The libraries were augmented by donations. Reading became fashionable, and our people having no public amusements to divert their attention from study became better acquainted with books. In a few years they were observed by strangers to be better instructed and more intelligent than people of the same rank generally are in other countries."

How much he loved to talk about his projects! There were many others that came out of the fertile minds of Franklin and his friends, though they are too numerous to mention in this space.

Now, dear reader, let me return to my point–an association of several people meeting together for mutual self improvement is an idea that people can apply in their own lives, regardless of their present station or circumstances.

To illustrate, allow me to inform you more fully of how his Junto functioned in their weekly Friday evening meetings. Again, I will use his exact words: "The rules I drew up required that every member in his turn should produce one or more queries on any point of morals, politics or natural philosophies to be discussed by the company, and once in three months, produce and read an essay of his own writing on any subject he pleased. Our debates were to be under the direction of a president and to be conducted in the sincere spirit of inquiry after truth, without fondness for dispute or desire for victory."

He told me the names of the original men who made up the study group. They included Joseph Breintnal, whose trade I do not at this time recollect; Thurman Godfrey, a self-taught mathematician and the inventor of what is now called Hadlers Quadrant; Nicholas Scull, a surveyor; William Parsons, originally a shoemaker and later acquired considerable skills in mathematics; William Maugridge, a joiner, a most exquisite man and a good, sensible person; Hugh Meredith; Stephen Potts; George Webb; Robert Grace, a young gentleman of some fortune, generous, witty, a lover of punning; and William Coleman, who according to Franklin, had the coolest head of anyone he ever knew.

This group, with the exception of one man who was quite contentious and was, therefore, soon asked to leave the group, met together for almost forty years. Yet the fact that I find most fascinating about this true story is that each of these men not only found significant success in their business ventures, but they also each became an outstanding contributor to the colonies. And each credited their achievements to the relationships and support of the group of which they were a part for so long.

Dr. Franklin admitted that he stumbled over a success principle with this group. He discovered a power at work that few people ever uncover or understand, though it is a force that anyone can harness and allow to carry them to higher levels of achievement and prosperity. Yet he also admitted, and I agree, that we actually have very little understanding of this great power or force, of people's minds joining together and mutually forming a new, more powerful common force. Undoubtedly, someday someone will more fully understand and articulate this strength that men get from one another, and then they will able to perfect and measure this force. In the meantime, I will try to describe it as best I can.

Let me begin by saying that it has been my observation that when two or more people or forces work together in a positive, harmonious way there arises out of that union a power that is greater than the sum of the individual powers. The key words in this statement are "positive" and "harmonious." Unless joint efforts embody these ingredients, they fight and devour each other, rather than complement each other. In order for such a group to be successful, it must be acknowledged that power is derived when people work together in a spirit of harmony, mutual support and encouragement, toward a common purpose. Power is negated when people work together in a spirit of conflict, a lack of harmony, or toward conflicting goals.

Any farmer who has hitched horses to a plow understands this principle. Animals that pull together as a team do work more easily than those that go in different directions. Once, while I was attending a harvest festival in the Pennsylvania countryside, I watched as a group of farmers demonstrated the power of their fine plow horses. One of the contests in which they engaged the beasts involved loading one hundred pound sacks of grain onto a huge wooden sled. One of the horses pulled it a predetermined distance, then its opponent pulled the same distance in the opposite direction.

After each had a successful turn, more sacks were added to the sled, until one by one the horses that were unable to pull the heavy sled were eliminated. To my amazement, the giant animal that pulled the most weight and, therefore, won first place, pulled just over 9,000 pounds, and close on his heels was the second place horse that pulled just a bit under that total.

After the winner was recognized, someone with a keen sense of competition called out this challenge: "Let's see how much those horses can pull together."

The crowd responded enthusiastically, laying down their wagers amid their roars of support for the contest.

As logical argument would lead one to expect, most of the bets were around 18,000 pounds. However, when both horses were hitched to one with the second sled hitched behind the first one, together they pulled them with ease. So more sacks of grain were added, and they again pulled the sled with ease. It was then necessary to add a third sled piled with sacks. Finally, when the two horses could pull no more, the three sleds were calculated to weigh over 30,000 pounds!

Please be assured dear reader, that is a true story.

Now, let us examine why these horses were able to achieve a feat like this. Please remember the following principle: When two or more people or forces work together in a spirit of unity and harmony toward a common goal, there arises a power that is much greater than the sum of the individual powers. When these horses worked together, they were able to almost double their pulling power.

Most highly prosperous people understand that this principle holds as true for people as it does for animals. On the other hand, many otherwise capable people fail because they do not understand this law well enough to let it work for them.

My purpose for writing this chapter, dear reader, is to introduce this great law and to suggest ways that you can take advantage of it. First, let me remind you of the power in my advice that you choose to associate with successful people. When you are with them, listen to them, learn from them, and open your mind to the wisdom that their years of experience has taught them.

Next, look for associates and people with whom you can function in a spirit of harmony and cooperation. As much as possible avoid people who are contentious and disagreeable. If you are looking for a spouse or mate, look for someone who will support you, who will recognize your better traits, and will give more attention to your strengths than to your weaknesses.

Since through inspiration the scriptures say, "It is more blessed to give than to receive," look for specific ways you can support others. Find ways you can help them discover and build on their own strengths. Avoid giving attention only to their weaknesses because in giving notice of them you often strengthen those faults within that person.

Grow in the grace of overlooking and forgiving others of their faults and offenses against you. Return not anger for anger, bitterness for bitterness, insult for insult. Be above all rancor. Seek to discover the best in people, to believe in their goodness.

When I was a young tradesman, beginning to build my enterprises, I quickly learned that I would only be as successful as the people who I attracted to work in my business. And, I am pained to say, I made many mistakes, but fortunately I was able to learn from them. I, at first, thought that I could build people by identifying their weaknesses, pointing them out, and thus causing their flaws to be corrected within them. I was to quickly learn that this was not a wise course to follow. I discovered that when I attempted to correct someone's weak habits that I often caused them to become weaker. It was like I was convincing them that they were in fact inadequate.

In due course I came to believe that the best way to build people and get them to practice positive, productive actions is to overlook, as much as possible, their weaknesses, and build on their positive traits. Yes, I know there are people who must be confronted for certain unacceptable behaviors. It is important during these times of confrontation to deal with the behaviors of the person and not the worth of the person.

I learned over the years that when I focus on successful behaviors in my people, they not only feel better about themselves, but they want to work more diligently for me. I soon discovered that the behaviors I chose to notice and reward in people were behaviors I would then see grow within them. I also learned my own expectations often preceded like actions of people.

Learning these valuable lessons helped me build strong, positive habits and traits in people. I later taught these principles to all my managers. It played no little part in the enormous success with which I have been blessed.

There is another extremely important principle I have learned, that of creating a positive ambiance in the place of employ. I observed that people will be far more productive, happy and fulfilled when they work as part of an organization in which they are valued and appreciated for their work. I am constantly amazed at the lack of wisdom of employers who drive and threaten their people and push them to work. I consider this practice very short-sighted and not conducive to the ongoing success of a business.

So, dear reader, allow me to summarize my thoughts. First, select your friends and associates carefully. Choose positive, supportive ones and you will help assure yourself a prosperous future. Recognize that if you choose or allow negative associates into your life, this will help insure your low achievement. Select the quality of life you want most to enjoy, then seek out people who already enjoy that quality of life. Ask to learn from them. Spend time with them. Observe their every action, habit and attitude. Model your actions after theirs, and one day, as day follows night, you will find that you have grown more like them.

Next, create a positive ambiance in your place of employ. Choose to see your people's stronger traits, and as you focus on them and reward them you will indeed help them to strengthen them. I have been very successful in building strong people this way.

Yes, as the wise Ben Franklin told me many years ago, "Associate with people who enjoy the level of success you would like to enjoy, and soon you will enjoy that level of prosperity yourself."

There are few principles of success and achievement that I value higher than this advice.

The Ninth Law of Wealth and Abundance

CHOOSE TO ASSOCIATE WITH SUCCESSFUL PEOPLE

Select the quality of life you want to enjoy, then look for people who enjoy this same quality and who reach goals you would like to reach. Ask to learn from them. Recognize that successful people are usually willing to help those who sincerely want to learn. Listen to their advice without bias. Observe their attitudes, habits, and ways of handling situations. Identify and develop their habits within yourself. Be careful with whom you associate. Realize the power your spouse, family, friends and associates have over you. Bring positive, supportive people into your life. Release negative, nonsupportive people as often as you can. Forgive and build others; this increases the positive flow of prosperity through your life. Remember that when two or more people or forces work in a united, harmonious way, toward common goals, the resulting power is greater than the sum of the individual ones.

Chapter 10

The Tenth Law of Wealth and Abundance

INCREASE YOUR WEALTH BY SHARING IT

Although the Almighty has so generously extended my years beyond one's normal life span, I continue to be a diligent seeker of knowledge. I have learned much about the accumulation of wealth which I feel compelled to share with anyone who is a serious student. I also persist in my search for understanding about life—its purpose and meaning—its complexities and mysteries.

Among the many truths I have witnessed is that wealth is not his who has it, but his who joyfully shares it.

I admit that I, like many of my colleagues, did not understand this paradox when I first began my quest for wealth and prosperity. Looking back, I am not sure I would have even recognized this truth had someone shared it with me in my younger years. Nor would I have put much stock in it. My observation is that this secret lies hidden from us until by diligent search and experience we stumble across it.

In this small volume, dear reader, I have written much about wealth, especially about its physical equivalents, the way most people measure it, money, possessions, material things.

Sooner or later, however, the person whose quest is for wealth discovers that he or she can only use so much money, that in seven days of a week a person can wear only a limited number of clothes or can eat only so much food. That, finally, one has no need for larger homes, carriages, or barns.

I realized years ago that once my family's needs were satisfied and we had a reasonable surplus set aside, my motives for making money changed. Realizing this, I observed people of means to see how attaining a comfortable level of wealth influenced their motivations and desires. I was at first perplexed by how I saw money change people's lives.

After gaining a surplus of money, some people remained the same, with no recognizable change in their values or habits. Others became more cruel, arrogant and self-centered. Still others became benevolent and sensitive to the needs of others. And with all these observations, I always asked myself, "Why? Why did wealth cause these people to become as they are?"

As I observed people I, in time, discovered that wealth soon reveals the true character of people. Wealth ruins some people, while it ennobles others. It often divides brothers from brothers, friends from friends, neighbors from neighbors. For some it leads to pride and self-destruction; for others it leads to wisdom and productiveness.

Such a paradox!

I have also come to believe that wealth often spoils those who are not prepared to receive it, who have not struggled and forged emotional muscles in the crucible of discipline and honest toil.

I must admit that it was only after my youth had passed and my own wealth began to grow that I was ready to observe this in people. It seemed that as long as I was still struggling I was too blinded by my own challenges to really notice the experiences of others.

First I had to attain an understanding of my own motivations for wealth. In time I discovered that much of the reason for my diligent work was to provide luxuries for my beautiful Rebecca and then to leave wealth to our son Benjamin. To protect him from the struggles that I myself had endured.

However, as I witnessed other people of wealth bequeath large amounts of money to their children, I clearly observed more often than not it laid burdens on them they were not prepared to shoulder. So I began to think more deeply about my actions and motives.

This led me to question my intentions and my judgment. Would my good wife be able to make proper decisions about our wealth if I were to experience separation from this life? What about Benjamin? What would sudden wealth do to him? I pondered and wrestled with these perplexing questions. I was made to examine my values, to consider deeply what I thought was right and wrong. This eventually led me to recount the whole of my life experiences and what I had learned from them.

From this examination the inner workings of my mind flashed before me many moments of joy and happiness, as well as deep sadness and grief. Permit me, dear reader, to digress for a moment and recount some of my thoughts. There was the loss of what would have been two beautiful children, and then the sad diagnosis that Rebecca could no longer bear children, thus ending her dreams for more precious souls to grace our home and bless our family.

It seems that invading my contemplation are always memories of that awful day when, as my beautiful Rebecca was leaving the

Pennsylvania Hospital after doing volunteer work, a drunken carriage driver so recklessly ran her down, leaving her broken body lying lifeless in the street.

My whole world seemed brutally torn from me. I then experienced a depth of emptiness and grief I never before knew existed.

First came my anger at the carriage driver, then came a deep black melancholy, a total lack of any sense of meaning and understanding. The wealth that I was accumulating suddenly had no value compared to my loss. The huge rooms of our estate were void of their previous merriment. Their emptiness silently stabbing at my emotions. The love that had given me so much energy and motivation to succeed no longer sustained and filled me. It was gone, gone, never to return.

The pain was almost more than I could bear. Everything I touched and looked at brought back memories of her, and the debilitating throbbing seemed to be renewed with every experience. I was distressfully torn between my own self-pity and my attempts to comfort my son Benjamin, for his needs were even greater than mine. So I was torn between my love and concern for him and my own utter emptiness.

Never before had I been forced to search the depths of my spirit for meaning and answers. How could this have happened? Why was my most treasured gift of love suddenly snatched from me? Is there really a God? If there is, does He actually care about me? If He does, then why did He allow this awful event to take place—if indeed He allows or doesn't allow events like this to happen?

These questions dogged me day and night. My own wisdom failed to soothe the constant pain which burned into the very core of my soul. For a period I questioned my own existence. I felt so alone, so cheated, so valueless. But because I had no other choice but to keep on, I began to put my life back together again, to search for significance and purpose.

As my search proceeded I began to learn that my life had previously been directed toward the gaining of wealth, to only discover that having it healed no hurts and filled no voids in the emptiness of my shattered emotions. So I longed for deeper meaning, and I began a new search for greater understanding and wisdom. It was to take me through a wide range of emotional experiences before clarity began to evidence itself.

It often seemed the more I learned, the less I knew; the more I questioned, the less sure I was of my answers. This continued until I felt as if I once again had more questions than answers. I soon realized that, for any man, doubts and uncertainties often precede wisdom. Once I admitted that, I was able to foster my determination to find the truth. The more unsure I was of my answers, the more I longed to discover what lay beyond.

Although I was quite unprepared to hear it at the time, it was Dr. Franklin who years ago suggested to me a great source of wisdom, a source which had kept his mind afresh with new ideas. He said that one who desires to gain more knowledge of the ways of the world should follow the path of Solomon, who he perceived to be the wisest man who ever lived.

So remembering his previous urging, I began my study of the Biblical books of Proverbs and Ecclesiastes. I wanted to discover and understand that which is the chief value of life. I desired to learn of the supreme objective to which people should dedicate their lives. I longed to comprehend more about the meaning of life's many ups and downs—of pain and suffering, of joy and happiness.

I hungered for the revelation that would open my mind to life's mysteries and profound truths. So that when I came to the end of my life I would not look back in frustration and discover that I had not known how I should have lived it and directed it. What a waste indeed that would be!

And so I diligently read the words of King Solomon—the wisest, wealthiest man in the world. I read of the riches he possessed and marveled at the unprecedented elegance he enjoyed. I read from the Jewish historian Josephus, who wrote that each morning the King arose before sunup and went to a beautiful spot for his meditation. He was dressed each day in a white robe, and his attendants sprinkled gold dust in his hair. His chariot was overlaid with pure gold. His entourage flanked his chariot in a moving "V" formation, while he was positioned in the pocket. The horses, each a near-perfect animal, were all matched colors. Their drivers and armor bearers were the handsomest and most muscular young men in the country, and they were dressed in royal purple raiment.

I read of Solomon's thousand wives, how each one was prepared with oils and perfumes and spices for six months, just to go to him for one night. I read of his palace, his gardens, his treasures, of the kings and queens from all over the world who came to marvel at his wisdom and wealth.

Throughout all this reading I sought the answer to these questions: "What chief lessons did this man learn? What values did he embrace as he neared the end of his life?"

To find the answers I read the words that he himself wrote, the words of the Preacher, the son of David, King of Jerusalem:

Vanity of vanities, saith the Preacher, vanity of vanities; all is vanity.

What profit hath a man of all his labour which he taketh under the sun?

One generation passeth away, and another generation cometh: but the earth abideth forever.

The sun also ariseth, and the sun goeth down, and hasteth to the place where it arose.

The wind goeth toward the south, and turneth about unto the north; it whirleth about continually, and the wind returneth again according to his circuits.

All the rivers run into the sea; yet the sea is not full: unto the place from whence the rivers come, thither they return again.

All things are full of labour; man cannot utter it: the eye is not satisfied with seeing nor the ear filled with hearing.

The thing that hath been, it is that which shall be; and that which is done is that which shall be done: And there is no new thing under the sun.

Is there anything whereof it may be said, See, this is new? It hath been already of old time, which was before us.

There is no remembrance of former things; neither shall there be any remembrance of things that are to come with those that shall come after.

—Ecclesiastes, Ch. 1, v.2-11

After my first few readings, I was puzzled at the despondent tone of this wise man's writings. If he was so wise why was he so perplexed at life? I later realized I was looking for simple answers, yet no simple answers were to be found.

I recall how Solomon examined many things in his pursuit of wisdom and understanding. He examined pleasure, fine wine, great projects, and possessions. As he neared the end of his life, he looked back and concluded that man can do nothing better than to eat and drink and find satisfaction in his work. That, be he rich or poor in this world's goods, he can enjoy no greater satisfaction than this simple contentment.

I looked about me and found only a fortunate few who appeared to enjoy true contentment.

The poor rob themselves of it by thinking only of survival; their anxiety for tomorrow robs them of the joy of today. It escapes the wealthy because they put their trust in their possessions, which soon decay, disappear, or prove to be empty.

So, both the rich and the poor can deny themselves what they would most like to have by the choices they make and the attitudes they adopt.

Witnessing this, I strengthened my resolve to escape this self-defeating trap. I read from King Solomon's pen, "Whoever loves money never has money enough; whoever loves wealth is never satisfied with his income."

Reflection upon this statement caused me to question my motives for gaining wealth. At first I felt uncomfortable that I was indeed seeking an illusive fulfillment.

In time I was able to work through my discomfort and put my thinking in order. I began by asking myself, "Why do I want wealth?" At first my only answer was, "Because having it is nice, and people respect and recognize me."

I soon moved past such simple responses. I discovered within myself significant levels of pride. I recognized my need for people to hold me in esteem. I admitted the pleasure I got from owning nice things and having people see them.

My first years of wealth were centered upon gratifying my own personal needs. But I soon arrived at the point where I felt assured that others knew of my success, so my need for recognition soon vanished and no longer pushed me.

Then when I felt I had all the possessions I wanted, my values began to change. I began to look at life differently. I was left with a certain sense of emptiness when I finally discovered that to what I had given energies actually held no lasting significance or real fulfillment. My own pride made that a most difficult lesson to learn.

Then one day in my reading of Solomon, I finally discovered new meaning in the words of the wise man. I must have read these words hundreds of times before but somehow their meaning escaped me. In time and in my search to satisfy my emptiness, the words of Solomon seemed to jump off the page at me. It was as if they had been carefully hidden until that very day when they appeared to be the only ones on the page. That day I read:

One man gives freely, yet gains even more
Another withholds unduly, but comes to poverty.
A generous man will prosper;
He who refuses others will himself be refused.

For many days I pondered these words, then I resolved to test the concept. I set goals to not only contribute a larger percentage of my income to help those less fortunate, but also to assist in projects in our city that served the needs of people. To carry out these goals I became intimately involved with hospitals, schools of learning, and community-betterment institutions.

I then set about to give away a large part of that which I had been blessed. It was then that I began to feel an expanded joy of living. I began to learn that it is more happy to give than to receive, as the Master Teacher said.

Upon this discovery I soon took special notice of those who seemed to lead happy, contented lives. I noticed, almost without exception, they spent their time going about doing good. This intrigued me. I also noticed another ever so subtle, yet quite profound, difference: Those who went about doing good and who saw no need to boast of their good works seemed to be the happiest. I, too, desired to enjoy the zest and happiness they seemed to have.

As I began this act of giving away my wealth, I began to experience a new sense of joy and fulfillment.

Carefully, I selected organizations and charities which I felt would contribute to the betterment of people and cause our great new nation to be a better place in which to live. I enlisted the help of several wise people to help me make the most judicious bequests, favoring the infirm and the homeless.

It was in this that I experienced an exhilaration which had been kept from me until I turned my eyes from making money to helping people with what I had. I discovered that, although my charities were kept as private as possible, as I gave, my enterprises flourished with a whole new level of prosperity. Then one day I discovered an interesting paradox—the more I gave to charity, the more I was blessed with increased profits. This brought me to a strange crossroads in my life.

It was then I made a momentous decision to withdraw a sufficient amount of money to see me to the end of my days. To give my son Benjamin a considerable sum for his personal management. To put the balance of my personal fortune in a trust to be given out for schools of higher learning, hospitals, and libraries. Then to transfer my business enterprises to my loyal employees so they could have ownership. I apportioned this ownership according to their individual tenure, loyalty and contributions.

Within a year, all these proceedings of transfer were completed, and I had time for reflection.

This time allowed me to review my life and link causes with effects. It permitted me to trace the considerable wealth I had attained to the seeds which produced it. I plainly saw that it was our early habit of tithing our income, giving it to our church and the poor, which planted the seeds of prosperity within us. It was evident that the vast wealth bestowed upon us was the offspring of the early habit of giving.

Such a paradox! One that was carefully hidden from me until I gained sufficient wisdom to comprehend it.

As I have witnessed the affairs of many people I can plainly see that whatever we give away opens the doors for us to receive more; and whatever we withhold closes the doors and shuts out our future prosperity. It is by giving that we expand. It is by withholding that we constrict. I learned this paradox is indeed a law of life.

I have spent no small number of hours contemplating this enigma, as well as the compensation that people who followed this law unexpectedly enjoyed. This insight, too, played a major role in my quest for the supreme value of life, the secret of secrets. I had not yet found it, but my growth was in its direction. As I look back now I can see I was being prepared to one day embrace this knowledge.

As I began to use my own gifts for the betterment of people, I experienced new levels of energy and zest. At first, I provided money and material help for people. Then, as time went on, I discovered that if I shared ideas and learning with people and watched them apply these lessons to their lives, I enjoyed a whole new dimension of fulfillment.

It was a fine feeling to help feed a poor family, but it was quite another thrill to help them find ways of feeding themselves. To be self-sufficient after my resources had been used up. I reveled when I was able to help them develop new levels of courage and confidence in themselves. I witnessed over and over again that when people change their thoughts and expectations, they change their lives.

It became clear to me that the most enjoyable riches of life are ones which transcend money and material gain. I learned the thrill of helping people discover their inner strengths and take possession of their own lives. I discovered that many people never reach the point of taking complete responsibility for their own lives. Instead, they allow themselves to blame other people, or circumstances, or conditions for their lot.

I wanted to aid people to take their lives into their own hands and productively use the talents their Creator gave them. In my later years I was able to teach many people to take control of their lives and fortunes. After they assumed responsibility, I would encourage them to seek Divine guidance and direction through prayer and meditation. I had witnessed that when people are ready to be responsible for their lives, they also open the door for the Almighty to enter their hearts in a fuller way.

I, too, learned the problems of directing my own life. Illnesses, diseases, uncertainties, death, events I could not control, these all baffled me. I came to believe in the unseen, impenetrable mind of God that uses life and death as part of His plan to sustain the universe.

As I sorted through my values, I one day uncovered the simple, yet profound truth that while everything God has created is good and valuable, some things are temporary while other things are eternal. This revelation caused me to spend no little time categorizing all my own possessions, which I recognized were mostly all temporary.

I then admitted that my tangible wealth is neither good nor bad, and it is wrong to label it as such. The chief question I finally came to ask as I viewed the wealth I had attained was this: "Would it last? Would it pass away? What will grow old and decay and disintegrate? Or what will endure into eternity?"

I examined other things, too: Relationships, family, how I treated people, how I reacted toward life's circumstances. I thought how my pride, selfishness and ambition often caused me harm; and how faith, hope, and charity toward others enriched my life.

As I examined what I valued, I asked myself, "Are these transitory? Will they pass away?" Often my answer was an emphatic

"Yes!" But as I evaluated higher values such as love, joy, peace and asked myself, "Will they pass away?" My answer was a resounding "No! They are lasting!"

Yes! These values will last! They will last because they are eternal! Eternal things endure; others pass away.

This contemplation soon led me to ask the supreme question, "To what end shall I give my life? What is the supreme good to which my Creator desires I dedicate myself? What is the highest essence of who I am and why I am here?"

To answer my questions I searched the writings of wise people. I counseled with wise men who had transcended their needs for possessions and wealth and had searched for spiritual significance. I devoured the Scriptures. Over and over I read the thirteenth chapter of First Corinthians, wherein the Apostle Paul concludes by writing, "And now abideth faith, hope, charity, these three; but the greatest of these is charity."

My desires became more and more centered on growing in this virtue and helping people to discover these eternal truths themselves. I wanted to share the gifts of life, hope, optimism, self-discovery, love and self-reliance.

Mixed throughout all my days, though, were the haunting memories of the crushing loss of my Rebecca (may she rest in peace). My continued grief about her death was mysteriously blended with my new joys forming a strange bittersweet set of emotions.

I spent no little amount of time attempting to come to terms with these conflicting feelings. Slowly it dawned on me that Rebecca was not dead but had been transformed and was now experiencing an even higher state of glory and purpose.

It came to me in my awakening moments, one day, that somehow, in His infinite wisdom, the Almighty had said, "I love

Rebecca so much that I need her to help me on an even more important dimension."

With this understanding I was eventually able to climb out of my sadness and mend my broken spirit.

After seemingly interminable periods of anger and confusion, I found comfort in this image of her enhancing Heaven with her beauty. I envisioned her seeing the face of God, and in this state of perfection experiencing complete, total happiness. There were, of course, many nights when this scene brought me to tears. Each incident, however, left me emotionally drained, yet feeling cleansed, happy and with a greater understanding that everything does indeed fit perfectly into God's purpose.

In time, through this spiritual discernment, my values were changed forever.

It was also out of the pain and struggle of my search for the supreme purpose of life that I was one day to agree with the words of the wise man Solomon, who, summing up his lifetime of learning, wrote: "Let us hear the conclusion to the whole matter: Fear God and keep His commandments, for this is the whole duty of man."

I took this to mean that I respect and hold in awe this power, and to allow it to flow through me.

Now, as I complete this little book of instruction, most of my life is behind me; although I sincerely believe that Life is still ahead.

And so, dear reader, whomever and wherever you are, I have candidly shared with you the way to wealth contained in *The Ten Laws of Wealth & Abundance*. I have laid out a path, if you indeed follow, you will surely enjoy prosperity and security. And as you satisfy your basic needs of survival, safety and knowledge, you will gradually be ushered into a realization and desire to seek higher needs.

It is within this crucible of life wherein you will also forge your values and priorities. As you seek greater wisdom and understanding, you will ultimately ask the supreme questions, "What is life all about, and what is my ultimate purpose here?"

May blessings go with you as you sail through the stormy and often uncertain seas of this journey. As you experience the inevitable pains, joys, sorrows and pleasures of life, may you press forward toward your ultimate purpose and in every respect achieve your destiny.

May you enjoy True Abundance.

The Tenth Law of Wealth and Abundance

INCREASE YOUR WEALTH BY SHARING IT

To increase your wealth, begin now to share it. Commit yourself to the habit of giving ten percent of your income to your house of worship or charity. Give silently without any need for recognition. Nothing else so plants the seeds for your future prosperity as this habit. As you give you will begin to assess your values. You will ask yourself what is important and what is not—what is temporary and what endures? Give your time to worthy causes. Give yourself time each week for study and reflection. Give people word gifts, compliment them, encourage them, build them. Give people the gift of forgiveness. Give yourself the gift of thanksgiving, remembering that a thankful spirit turns all it touches into happiness. Give the Creator a space in your heart to dwell and to reveal His will for you.

EPILOGUE

Andrew Baldwin celebrated his eightieth birthday in 1825, as his maturing nation was struggling for its identity. Many changes had taken place in the previous quarter century. Led by brave pioneers, the United States of America grew and spread west. In the East, cities rose up in anticipation of the great industrial revolution years which lay just ahead.

The decade 1790 to 1800, a time of vast national transition, of settling in, was one of the richest periods in this nation's history. It was said by some that greater transitions and changes took place during this decade than in the first ninety years of the century combined.

On April 17, 1790, Benjamin Franklin's full life ended. During his eighty-four years he had achieved more than anyone else on this sleeping giant of a continent. His gifts to government and foreign relations were legion.

In tribute, twenty thousand Philadelphians followed the cortege to his grave. An old enemy, William Smith, provost of the University of Pennsylvania, gave his eulogy in Christ Church. One well-known city figure remarked that Franklin's death severed the tie with colonial America and ushered in a new era. History was indeed changed forever by the life of this one man.

Andrew Baldwin's public works, although less publicized than Franklin's, were also numerous. Retiring soon after he turned sixty and in time disposing of his business interests, Andrew spent his last years involved in charitable causes.

From Boston to New York City and from Philadelphia to the settlement which became known as Washington, D.C., he contributed to many public works and charities. He established hospitals, public libraries and schools. His estate above the Schuylkill

River became the center for a great university. He helped begin the Pennsylvania Academy of the Fine Arts at Broad and Cherry Streets in 1805, and to this institution he donated several priceless pieces of art.

Able to sense the needs of the future, Andrew helped Alexander Hamilton establish the banking system of the young country. He fought hard to encourage the use of paper currency, backed by gold bullion in the federal treasuries. He believed that a strong banking system was fundamental to a strong nation.

In 1806, a new hospital grew out of the famed Pennsylvania Hospital, founded in 1756 by Franklin and a few influential friends. Its cornerstone read, "For the Relief of the Sick and Miserable." A whole wing of this magnificent new facility was named after Rebecca Baldwin.

As the city had grown, so had the needs of health care. Andrew Baldwin, sensing this demand, contributed one-half of the cost of the new wing and, to further show his spirit of benevolence, offered to lead the fund-raising campaign for the balance. It took only two months to raise the rest of the money for the whole project.

It was in that hospital in the year 1816 that a brilliant, thirty-nine-year-old chief physician and surgeon who had been expertly trained by Dr. William Shippin, Jr., professor of anatomy and surgery at the College of Philadelphia, made a simple but lifesaving medical breakthrough. He demonstrated that by simply requiring all the nurses and physicians to wash their hands in a chlorine solution before surgery and delivery, the maternal mortality rate in the hospital could be reduced from a staggering thirty-eight percent to an incredibly low two percent. As a result, thousands of mothers were spared the tragic death previously inevitable for so many.

In his lifetime, this brilliant physician, Benjamin Baldwin, reaped great renown for this and other innovations in medicine. Widely recognized for his brilliance and astuteness, he also worked closely with the famed Dr. Casper Wistar and conducted many experiments with a revolutionary process called vaccination.

Andrew Baldwin's last years were blessed with much joy and fulfillment. He was able to spend rich segments of time with his grandchildren, Jonathan and Anna-Rebecca, during their growing years, and to take pleasure in the love and companionship Benjamin and his wife Elisabeth enjoyed.

And now, as his way of paying back for the vast levels of prosperity he enjoyed, Andrew Baldwin has shared these *Ten Laws of Wealth and Abundance* with you, so you may enjoy the level of prosperity of your choosing.

And finally, let it be known that the diligent practice of these ten laws can liberate people from the shackles of poverty and hopelessness and elevate them to unparalleled levels of fulfillment, wisdom and prosperity.

Ron Willingham is the author of twelve books. Among them are *Integrity Selling For The 21st Century, The Inner Game of Selling, Integrity Service, Hey, I'm The Customer*, and, *The You, You Never Knew*.

He has written over thirty training and development courses that have been conducted in eighty nations. In excess of 27,000 people have been certified to conduct them, with upwards to 2,000,000 graduates. Some of his courses are: *Integrity Selling®, Integrity Coaching®, Managing Goal Achievement®, The Way to Wealth™*, and *Money2Spare™*.

He helped found Kids at Hope, a national non-profit organization–working through schools, Boys & Girls Clubs, and YMCAs, training caring adults to help kids succeed in their lives.

If You Enjoyed This Book...

And would like to integrate the prosperity building concepts into your life, you'll want to know more about our courses:

- The Ten Laws of Wealth & Abundance Seminar. A half day seminar that helps you set specific personal and financial goals, and a strategy to reach them. You'll also benefit by a ten-week self or group study process.
- The Way to Wealth™ is a nine-week intensive course that changes the way you view money. You'll learn why you have or don't have what you want out of life. This dynamic life skills course will completely change your financial future.
- Money2Spare™ is an online course that helps individuals set and achieve personal, career, and financial goals.

Learn How To Become A Certified Facilitator For Our Seminar and Courses

We are certifying qualified people to conduct our learning process in organizations and as a career opportunity.

For more information visit:
www.LifeScriptLearning.com
www.TheWaytoWealth.com
www.TheTenLawsofWealth.com
www.Money2Spare.com